Cc

ITALY

ALBANIA

BOSNIA HERZEGOVINA

BULGARIA

GREECE

CORFU

Ionian Islands

Aegean Sea

Athens

Ionian Sea

HarperCollins*Publishers*

YOUR COLLINS TRAVELLER

Your Collins Traveller Guide will help you find your way around your chosen destination quickly and simply. It is colour-coded for easy reference:

The blue section answers the question 'I would like to see or do something; where do I go and what do I see when I get there?' This section is arranged as an alphabetical list of topics. It is recommended that an up-to-date atlas or street plan is used in conjunction with the location maps in this section. Within each topic you will find:
- A selection of the best examples on offer.
- How to get there, costs and opening times for each entry.
- The outstanding features of each entry.
- A simplified map, with each entry plotted and the nearest landmark or transport access.

The red section is a lively and informative gazetteer. It offers:
- Essential facts about the main places and cultural items.
  What is La Bastille? Who was Michelangelo? Where is Delphi?

The gold section is full of practical and invaluable travel information. It offers:
- Everything you need to know to help you enjoy yourself and get the most out of your time away, from Accommodation through Baby-sitters, Car Hire, Food, Health, Money, Newspapers, Taxis and Telephones to Youth Hostels.

PRICES (1993)	Inexpensive	Moderate	Expensive
Attractions			
Museums, etc.	200-300 Drs	400-500 Drs	over 600 Drs
Restaurants			
Meal, exc. wine	1000-1500 Drs	1500-3000 Drs	over 3000 Drs
Nightclubs			
Entry and drink	under 1000 Drs	1000-2000 Drs	2000-5000 Drs

Cross-references:

Type in small capitals – CHURCHES – tells you that more information on an item is available within the topic on churches.

A-Z after an item tells you that more information is available within the gazetteer. Simply look under the appropriate name.

A name in bold – **Holy Cathedral** – also tells you that more information on an item is available in the gazetteer – again simply look up the name.

CONTENTS

CONTENTS

▨ PRACTICAL INFORMATION GAZETTEER

INTRODUCTION

Corfu is still, in the late 20thC, as beguiling as ever. The crescent-shaped island can still bewitch – as it did Homer and Shakespeare – despite all the attendant, sometimes overbearing, interest that its fine features attract. In *The Tempest* (Act II, Scene 1) Shakespeare evoked its 'subtle, tender and delicate temperance . . . How lush and lusty the grass looks! How green!' If you climb into a pine wood in the island's interior it might just be possible to imagine things haven't changed much since. Of course, they have changed dramatically. The pub, disco and taverna culture along the bustling east coast is beloved by the British, and the resorts of Benitses and Kavos vibrate to a young, pop beat.

This Ionian island, about 96 km by 40 km, attracts young tourists and is visited by more British holiday-makers than any other Greek island. It has a strangely green look, its verdant slopes being in dramatic contrast to the sparse vegetation of bustling Mykonos or Santorini in the Cyclades away to the southeast. You can find slopes carpeted in wild flowers, hills laden with cypresses, and orange and lemon groves. The predominant tree is the olive, on which the island's Venetian conquerors once based a thriving economy. Today the Corfiots make money out of the tourists who come each summer to worship the sun.

Despite the rich overlays of cultures which once fought and squabbled over the island, it retains no architectural wonders, yet it still has many legacies of past rulers. Kerkyra, the name given to the island by the Dorians of Corinth, the first settlers, has had an astonishingly turbulent passage to the 20thC. Although it may be hard to imagine today, the island was once an important, rich land at the centre of western civilization. In the 14thC the Venetians took over the island. They fought bitterly with the Turks in the 16thC and finally lost possession of Corfu two centuries later to Napoleon and the French. Following Napoleon's defeat, the Ionian islands were put under the protectorate of Britain and Corfu became the seat of the High Commissioner. In 1864 the islands were restored to the Greeks. More recently, Corfu was bombed by the Italians in 1923 and by the Germans in 1940. Corfu's affair with the tourist is a relatively recent phenomenon – and, some believe, an ill-fated one.

But Corfu has two jewels which have not been drastically altered by the invading Euro-tourists. The most celebrated is Paleokastritsa, the real beauty spot on Corfu. Lawrence Durrell, a great fan of the island (his book

Prospero's Cell is about Corfu), once noted that, despite recent developments, Paleokastritsa remained 'a dream place'. It is one of those magical Greek places for sitting, sipping drinks and watching a giant sun sink into the sea. The sky will change colour a hundred times before the last cocktail has been downed, and the last picture snapped. There is also a string of beautiful pebble and sand coves along the coast, nestling beneath steep, rocky cliffs to which olives and cypresses stubbornly cling. Choose this resort on Corfu and you will have little reason to be disappointed.

The second jewel is Corfu Town itself, a picturesque, cosmopolitan city which can be educational, chic and laid-back all in the space of a few attractive cobbled streets. Sit in a street café in Theotoki Square, surrounded by foreign babble and baubles, and watch the world pass by on the back of every form of two-wheeled transport imaginable. Families of four can get on one scooter; motorcycles bear dark, tousle-haired guys with long-legged girls hanging on behind them. Traffic in Corfu Town is all gesticulation, braking and honking of horns.

The city is at its most attractive around the Palace of St. Michael and St. George, the Old Fort, and along the Spianada, which climbs past neo-classical buildings from the quayside and the ferry terminals towards the old part of the city. Corfu boasts attractive parks, good restaurants,

cafés and boutiques, and has a cross-European atmosphere which you are unlikely to find in other parts of the island. Unless you have to be on a beach, it's well worth basing your holiday in Corfu Town and using a hired car for the rest of the island.

Wherever you stay, you should arrive knowing that you will not find Shakespeare's isle, or even Durrell's isle, but an island which has been transformed by tourism and sometimes insensitive development. However, you can be sure that its climate and lively image will keep on attracting visitors. And, with a little bit of effort, you may find your own ideal somewhere on Kerkyra and discover why the island has been fought over so often.

Benitses

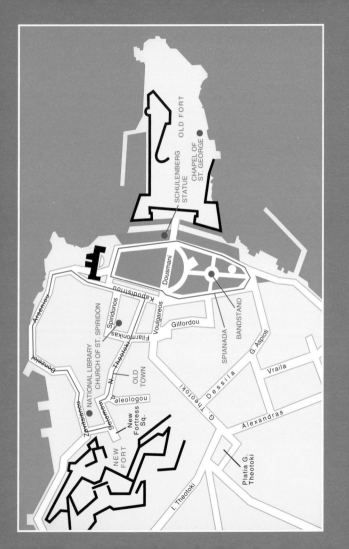

Corfu Town

OLD TOWN *North of N. Theotoki, a mass of tiny streets, some stepped and mostly paved with uneven slabs of marble. Washing hangs from upper windows, cats snooze in doorways, bougainvillea drips over walls and old ladies in black sit at windows watching the passers-by.*

CHURCH OF ST. SPIRIDON Old Town.
◈ Free but donations invited.
The spiritual centre of the island, with relics of the patron saint. See **Events, St. Spiridon**.

OLD FORT On eastern promontory of the town.
▨ 0800-1900. ◈ Inexpensive.
Venetian fortress which once housed the entire population. See **A-Z**.

CHAPEL OF ST. GEORGE Old Fort.
▨ 0800-1900. ◈ Fee payable at entrance to Old Fort. Inexpensive.
Originally an Anglican garrison chapel, restored after World War II.

NEW FORT Tenedou Street, above the port.
▨ 0800-1900. ◈ Inexpensive.
Fabulous views of the town and to the mainland from the top.

NATIONAL LIBRARY At the entrance to New Fortress Square.
▨ 0900-1400. ◈ Free.
Built by Lord Guilford as a study centre for poets. Now a public library.

SPIANADA In front of the Old Fort.
Esplanade and elegant French-style arcade (The Listons). See **Sports**.

BANDSTAND At southern end of Spianada.
Built in memory of Sir Thomas Maitland (see **High Commissioners**).

SCHULENBERG STATUE Central Avenue, just before entering the Old Fort.
The statue commemorates a German mercenary, hired by the Venetians, who successfully defended the town against the Turks in 1716.

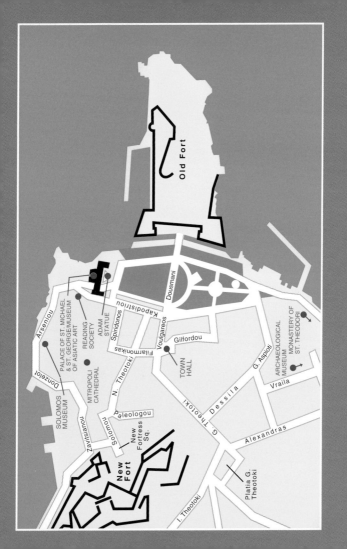

PALACE OF ST. MICHAEL & ST. GEORGE (ROYAL PALACE) Spianada. ▧ Closed to the public for renovation.
*Staterooms, the Museum of Asiatic Art, and the public library. See **A-Z**.*

MUSEUM OF ASIATIC ART Palace of St. Michael & St. George.
▧ Closed for renovation. *Outstanding collection of Sino-Japanese art at present (1993) without a home but due to be rehoused shortly. See **A-Z**.*

ADAM STATUE In front of the Palace of St. Michael & St. George.
*Statue of Sir Frederick Adam (see **High Commissioners**), curiously attired in a toga.*

TOWN HALL Voulgareos Square.
*A lovely Venetian building in an attractive square. See **A-Z**.*

MITROPOLI CATHEDRAL Mitropoleos Square.
▧ 0800-1330, 1630-2030. ● Free. *The Greek Orthodox Cathedral of St. Theodora Augusta is an imposing Byzantine-inspired building in a pretty square with cafés and fountains. The silver reliquary containing the saint's remains is opened annually.*

ARCHAEOLOGICAL MUSEUM 1 Vraila Street.
▧ 0830-1500 Tue.-Sun. ● Moderate, Free on Sun. Fee for photography.
*Corfu's history told through artefacts from local excavations. See **A-Z**.*

SOLOMOS MUSEUM 41 Arseniou Street.
▧ 1700-2000 Mon. & Wed.-Fri. ● Inexpensive.
Museum dedicated to Dyonysis Solomos, Greece's national poet.

READING SOCIETY 120 Kapodistriou Street. ▧ 0900-1400. ● Free.
Books, manuscripts and prints on Ionian history and culture.

MONASTERY OF ST. THEODORI Stratia, off the Kanoni road.
▧ 0800-1330, 1600-1930. Bus 2. ● Free but donations invited.
*An active monastery laid out around a peaceful courtyard. There are early archaeological sites nearby in Stratia (see **ATTRACTIONS 3**).*

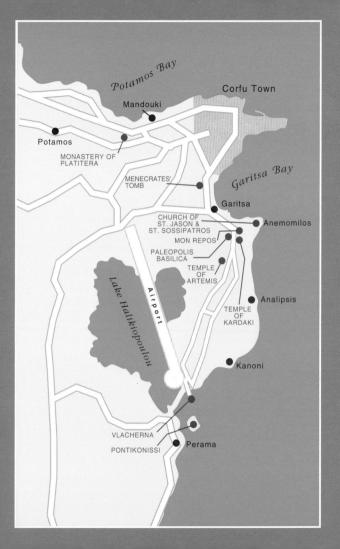

Corfu District

MON REPOS 1.5 km south of Corfu Town centre. Bus 2 from Esplanade. ■ House closed to the public; free access to grounds.
A delapidated 19thC villa, the birthplace of Prince Philip in 1921.

PALEOPOLIS BASILICA Opposite gates of Mon Repos. ● Free.
Remains of one of the oldest churches in Corfu, built around the 5thC AD. On the other side of the road are the remains of a Roman bath.

CHURCH OF ST. JASON & ST. SOSSIPATROS In the centre of Anemomilos, at the southern end of Garitsa Bay.
A small 12thC Byzantine church of much interest. See **A-Z**.

MONASTERY OF PLATITERA Near the suburb of Mandouki.
17thC monastery with examples of rare post-Byzantine icons. See **A-Z**.

VLACHERNA At southern end of Kanoni promontory. Bus 2 from Esplanade. ● Free but donations invited.
Walk out to this beautifully kept 17thC convent and chapel on a narrow causeway. Boats run from here to Pontikonissi.

PONTIKONISSI Kanoni Bay, 3 km south of Corfu Town. Bus 2 from Esplanade then short boat trip. ● Inexpensive.
Also known as Mouse Island, this islet is capped by trees and a small church and has featured in myriad postcards and snapshots.

MENECRATES' TOMB 0.5 km south of Corfu Town, behind Garitsa Bay off V. Konstantinou. ● Free.
Circular stone base which used to support a crouching lion (now in the Archaeological Museum – see **A-Z***), dating from the 7thC BC.*

TEMPLE OF ARTEMIS Stratia, off the Kanoni road. Bus 2 from Esplanade. ● Free.
One of Corfu's most important temples. See **Archaeological Museum**.

TEMPLE OF KARDAKI On seaward side of Mon Repos. ● Free.
Remains of a large hill-top sanctuary, probably dedicated to Hera.

MONASTERY OF PALEOKASTRITSA 24 km northwest of Corfu Town. ▥ 0700-1300, 1500-2000. Bus from New Fort Bus Station. ⊕ Free but donations invited.
13thC Byzantine monastery. See EXCURSION 2, **Paleokastritsa**.

ANGELOKASTRO 24 km northwest of Corfu Town, via Krini. Paleokastritsa bus from New Fort Bus Station then walk. ⊕ Free.
13thC Byzantine castle on a rocky headland. See **Paleokastritsa**.

MOUNT PANTOCRATOR 35 km northwest of Corfu Town. Turn left after Pyrgi to Strinilas, then take very rough road to the top (906 m). ⊕ Free. *Chapel and remains of 14thC monastery, and transmitting station with tremendous views. See* EXCURSION 1.

PERITHIA 46 km northwest of Corfu Town. 2-3 buses per day from Kassiopi. *On the slopes of Mount Pantocrator, this almost deserted village has winding, cobbled streets.*

KASSIOPI 36 km northeast of Corfu Town. Bus from New Fort Bus Station. *Historic harbour, ruined castle, and church with 17thC frescoes. See* BEACHES 1, EXCURSION 1, **A-Z**.

HISTORY & FOLKLORE MUSEUM OF CENTRAL CORFU Sinarades. ▥ 0930-1430 Tue.-Sun. ⊕ Inexpensive. *A village house left in original state, with mill, local costumes and remains of a papyrus boat.*

MORAITIKA & MESSONGHI 19 km south of Corfu Town. Kavos bus from New Fort Bus Station. *There are early Greek temples in the hills around Messonghi and a Roman bath in Moraitika.*

ACHILLION PALACE Gastouri, 8 km south of Corfu Town. ▥ 0800-1800. Bus 10 from San Rocco Square. ⊕ Moderate.
Summer residence of the Empress Elizabeth. See EXCURSION 2, **A-Z**.

AGIOS MARKOS 16 km north of Corfu Town, near Pyrgi. ⊕ Free. *Built in 1075 with Cappadocian-style frescoes. See* EXCURSION 1.

East & North Coasts

DASSIA 13 km northwest of Corfu Town. Bus 7 from San Rocco Square. *Wide bay with narrow, pebbly beach. Water sports at camp sites and hotels.*

IPSOS 16 km northwest of Corfu Town. Kassiopi bus from New Fort Bus Station. *Long, narrow stretch of beach. Hotels, camp sites and lively nightlife. See* EXCURSION 1.

BARBATI 18 km north of Corfu Town. Kassiopi bus from New Fort Bus Station. *Lovely long pebbly beach a short walk down through olive groves. Quiet.*

NISSAKI 23 km north of Corfu Town. Kassiopi bus from New Fort Bus Station. *Delightful small bay with wonderfully clear blue water. Beach hotel. See* EXCURSION 1.

KALAMI 30 km north of Corfu Town. Kassiopi bus from New Fort Bus Station. *Beautiful small bay with narrow, stony beach, once home to Lawrence Durrell. Readers of* Prospero's Cell *will recognize the area. Tavernas. See* EXCURSION 1.

KASSIOPI 36 km north of Corfu Town. Bus from New Fort Bus Station. *Pretty harbour backed by busy resort with a shingle beach. Boats to nearby Kalamaki and Agios Spiridon. See* EXCURSION 1, **A-Z**.

RODA 38 km northwest of Corfu Town. Bus from New Fort Bus Station. *Sprawling but low-key resort with a crescent of sandy beach. See* EXCURSION 1.

ASTRAKERI 36 km northwest of Corfu Town. Best reached by car, or walk about 2.5 km from Roda. *Quiet but rather exposed beach with a hotel and taverna.*

SIDARI 35 km northwest of Corfu Town. Bus from New Fort Bus Station. *Long beach of soft, almost red, sand, backed by many kilometres of tawdry development. See* EXCURSION 3.

West Coast

AGIOS GEORGIOS BAY 35 km northwest of Corfu Town. By road via Troumpeta and Pagi; by boat from Paleokastritsa. *Wide, sandy, relatively isolated beach becoming increasingly popular. See* EXCURSION 3.

PALEOKASTRITSA 26 km northwest of Corfu Town. Bus from New Fort Bus Station. Boats to more inaccessible coves. *Busy resort with beautiful scenery and some delightful coves. See* EXCURSION 2, **A-Z**.

ERMONES 15 km west of Corfu Town. Vatos/Glyfada bus from New Fort Bus Station. *Sandy beach with the usual rash of development. See* EXCURSION 2.

MYRTIOTISSA 16 km west of Corfu Town. Walk from Ermones or Pelekas; by boat from Ermones, Glyfada or Paleokastritsa. *Sheer cliffs, sandy beach, crystal water. Unofficial nudist beach.*

GLYFADA 17 km west of Corfu Town, below Pelekas village. Bus from New Fort Bus Station. *Beautiful sandy beach suitable for everyone. Facilities at beach hotel. See* EXCURSION 2.

AGIOS GORDIOS 26 km southwest of Corfu Town. Agios Gordios/Sinarades bus from New Fort Bus Station. *Glorious sands framed by vineyards and sheer cliffs. See* EXCURSION 2.

AGIOS GEORGIOS–LAKE KORISSION 28 km south of Corfu Town. Kavos/Lefkimmi bus from New Fort Bus Station. By car: off Lefkimmi road at Linia for Korission; off 2 km after Linia for Agios Georgios. *Windswept, golden dunes. No shade or fresh water. Facilities at Agios Georgios.*

KAVOS 47 km southeast of Corfu Town. Bus from New Fort Bus Station. *Crowded young resort with long beach. Clear, shallow water.*

MESSONGHI 23 km south of Corfu Town. Bus from New Fort Bus Station; by car off the Lefkimmi road. *Clean sand, shallow water, but narrow and crowded. See* EXCURSION 2.

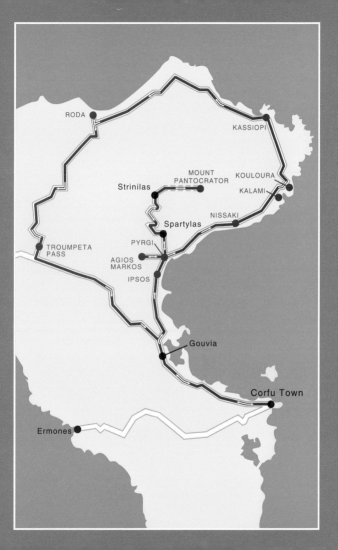

The North

A one-day excursion north from Corfu Town along the east coast and inland to Mount Pantocrator, the highest peak on the island (only attempt this diversion if you have a four-wheel drive vehicle).

Leave Corfu Town heading north, passing the still-beautiful bays of Gouvia and Dafnila.

15 km – Ipsos (see **BEACHES 1**). The remains of a fishing village are now at the heart of this highly developed stretch of coast where one town blends into the next. The local church here has 11thC frescoes.

16 km – Pyrgi. Amid the bars and discos, the 16thC Agios Pantocrator is worth a visit. Turn left at the end of the waterfront for Agios Markos (see **ATTRACTIONS 4**), a pretty 11thC church 2 km west of Pyrgi. There are spectacular views from the courtyard.

For a 38 km diversion to Mount Pantocrator, turn sharp left just beyond Pyrgi at the signpost for Spartylas (7 km). One kilometre after the village there is a signpost to Petali and Lefki. Turn right here for Strinilas (4 km). One kilometre beyond the village take the right-hand fork signposted to Pantocrator. The road becomes very rough after 1 km. You should walk from here (3 km, about 1 hr) unless you have a four-wheel drive vehicle.

25 km – Mount Pantocrator (see **ATTRACTIONS 4**). If it is not too hazy you should be able to see most of southern Corfu and across to the mainland. The 14thC monastery is abandoned, the cells empty and full of rubbish, with a

Kalami

huge transmitting station planted in the courtyard, but the chapel is well kept with polished brass and lighted candles. Make your way back to Strinilas, perhaps for an iced coffee in the shady taverna. Turn left when you rejoin the coast road.

59 km – Nissaki (see **BEACHES 1**). The coast road passes above the beach through this small resort with rooms to rent.

65 km – Kalami (see **BEACHES 1**) **& Kouloura** (2 km off the road). Either of these pretty bays will provide the perfect spot for a swim and lunch. Lawrence Durrell's White House at Kalami is now a guesthouse and taverna.

70 km – Kassiopi (see **ATTRACTIONS 4**, **BEACHES 1**, **A-Z**). The first city to be built here to take advantage of the fine natural harbour was founded in 300 BC, and there are ruins of a 13thC fortress overlooking the bay. Today there are still fishing boats tied up at the pretty waterfront alongside the tripper boats.

83 km – Roda (see **BEACHES 1**). The extensive sandy beach,

Troumpeta Pass

backed by rugged hills, has long made this a popular resort. Return to the crossroads outside Roda and take the Kerkyra (Corfu Town) road south through the Troumpeta Pass, giving spectacular views of the northern mountains and glimpses of the west coast. Below the pass turn left onto the main road for Corfu Town (20 km).

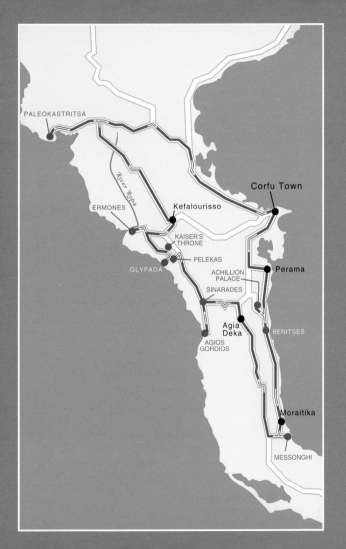

Paleokastritsa

A one-day excursion to some of the island's popular beaches and resorts.

Take the Lefkimmi road out of Corfu Town towards Benitses. At Vrio keep right, following signposts for Ahilio.

9 km – Gastouri. The Achillion Palace (see **ATTRACTIONS 4**, **A-Z**) is right at the top of the hill, through the village. Descend on the other side of the hill to the coast road and continue south.

12.5 km – Benitses. Another ex-fishing village and popular resort, with a pebble beach and some Roman remains. Drive through Moraitika. Where the main road bends sharp right, carry straight on for about 0.5 km and turn left after crossing the river.

22 km – Messonghi (see **BEACHES 2**). The road is bordered by old olive trees and leads to a clean, sandy beach, backed by hotels and apartments. Rejoin the main road and turn right after about 1 km, signposted Agia Deka. This narrow, winding road gives you glimpses of both coasts, passing through several quiet mountainside villages and lush valleys planted with olive and citrus trees. Rejoin the main road and turn left, signposted Sinarades.

45 km – Agios Gordios (see **BEACHES 2**). Another lovely beach, with a beautiful backdrop of sheer cliffs and fascinating rock formations. Rejoin the main road and drive north through Sinarades, where you can visit the History and Folklore Museum of Central Corfu (see **ATTRACTIONS 4**), following signs for Pelekas.

56 km – Pelekas. There are wonderful views from the hilltop. Wilhelm II used to watch the sunsets from the spot now known as Kaiser's Throne. Turn left here for the beach at Glyfada or continue on the main road to Paleokastritsa across the Plain of Ropa.

60 km – Glyfada (see **BEACHES 2**). This wide, sandy beach is backed by dunes and plenty of accommodation and cafés. Turn left just before Pelekas for Ermones.

65 km – Ermones (see **BEACHES 2**). A busy beach at the mouth of the River Ropa in the wild landscape where Odysseus is supposed to have met Nausicaa. The island's main golf course is nearby (see **Sports**). Rejoin the main road and turn left after 2 km. Turn left again at Kefalourisso for Paleokastritsa.

80 km – Paleokastritsa (see **ATTRACTIONS 4**, **BEACHES 2**, **A-Z**). This resort

Paleokastritsa

is set in some of the most attractive scenery on the island, with a Byzantine monastery and fortress perched on rocky headlands. Hidden coves can be reached by boat and there are plenty of tavernas to refresh you after a long drive. Stay here for the sunset and make your way back to Corfu Town by the direct route across the island (26 km).

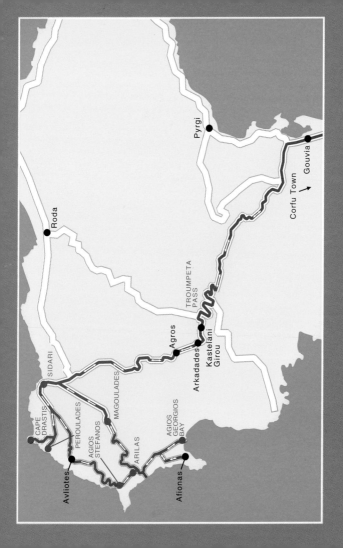

A one-day excursion to the remote northwest of the island.

Leave Corfu Town on the road going north, forking left after 5 km at Gouvia, signposted to Paleokastritsa. After 5 km turn right for Sidari (21 km) and climb up through the wooded hillsides to the Troumpeta Pass, which offers spectacular views of the mountains and to the sea. At 19 km keep left, following signs for Sidari. On the northern side of the pass, as you drive through the villages of Kastelani Girou, Arkadades and Agros, there are good views of the east coast. Stop and listen to the quietness, savour the shade of the olive trees, and watch the laden donkeys clip-clopping up the road, before descending to the coastal plain.

33 km – Sidari (see **BEACHES 1**). Drive through the appalling sprawl that is Sidari and after 3 km take the right fork to Peroulades.

38 km – Peroulades. Park and take the sharp turn to the right, signposted Cape Drastis. A 15 min walk will give you fabulous views of the cape, the islands offshore and the mainland. Another 10 min will take you to the headland itself. Return to the car and carry on through the village to the Panorama Restaurant at Longas Beach. The sandstone cliffs here are very soft and have been sculpted by the sea and wind into intricate bays and caves. The sea is shallow offshore, giving the water almost real turquoise tones. Return to the fork in the road outside Peroulades and turn right for Avliotes and Agios Stefanos.

49 km – Agios Stefanos. Keep going round the bay through the scattered development to the colourful little church. The terrace of the San Stefanos Hotel opposite is a pleasant spot for lunch, with views along the beach to the cliffs of the northwest corner. Keep right on your way out of the village and follow the coast road round to Arilas.

55 km – Arilas. This unsophisticated little beach resort is a good place to while away the afternoon, or you can continue to Afionas or Agios Georgios Bay (see **BEACHES 2**). Return to Arilas and keep right at the Agios Stefanos junction for Magoulades. There are potholes and some spectacular bends on this road, so take care.

60 km – Magoulades. From the Church of St. Theophilus there are views of the mountains. Do not be misled by the sign in the town for Kerkyra via Kavadades – this road is not suitable for most cars. Carry on to the main road outside Sidari and turn right for Corfu Town (30 km).

PAXOS

Boats from the Old Port, Corfu Town (3 hr). Pegassos: 1400 Mon., Tue., Thu. & Sat., 1500 Fri.; returns 1000 Mon., 0730 Tue. & Thu.-Sat. Zefiros: 1000 & 1800 Mon., 1430 Tue., Thu. & Sat., 1700 Fri., 1830 Sun.; returns 0700 & 1430 Mon., 1000 Tue., Thu. & Fri., 0700 Sat., 1600 Sun. Boat from Kavos leaves 0930 Mon., Tue., Fri. & Sat.
Tiny fertile island in lovely clear waters. Spectacular sea caves. See **A-Z**.

ANTIPAXOS

Boats from Gaios, Paxos. 0900-1100; returns 1430-1900 (40 min).
Off the Paxos coast. Sandy beaches, some accommodation. See **Paxos**.

LEFKADA

Bus from Athens to Patra (4 per day, 7 hr), then ferry. Boats from Ithaca (3 hr 30 min) and Kephalonia (4 hr 30 min) twice a week.
Separated from the mainland by a 25 m canal. Good beaches. See **A-Z**.

KEPHALONIA

Boats to Sami from Patra, mainland (2 per day, 4 hr); from Ithaca (daily, 1 hr 30 min); from Paxos (1 per week, 4 hr). Boats to Fiscardo from Vassiliki, Lefkada (2 per day, 3 hr); from Vathi, Ithaca (2 per day, 1 hr). Boats to mainland (Astakos and Mitikas) and Nidri (Lefkada) once a week July & Aug. Also ferries from Brindisi, Corfu and Igoumenitsa. Flights from Athens to Argostolion (Olympic Airways, 45 min).
Largest of the Ionian islands. Still unspoilt by the tourist trade. See **A-Z**.

ITHACA

Boats to Vathi from Patra, mainland and Sami, Kephalonia (daily, 6 hr and 1 hr 15 min); from Astakos, mainland (daily, 2 hr). Boats to Frikes from Lefkada (0900 daily, 4 hr); from Fiscardo, Kephalonia (1 hr).
Small rocky island with unspoilt scenery and lovely beaches. See **A-Z**.

ZAKINTHOS

Boats from Killini, mainland (6 per day, 1 hr 15 min); from Argostolion, Kephalonia (1200 Sun., 3 hr). Flights from Athens (Olympic Airways).
Beautiful, wild and mountainous. Limited accommodation. See **A-Z**.

CASINO Hilton Hotel, Kanoni.
▓ 2000-0200 (0300 Sat.). Bus 2 from Esplanade. ● Expensive.
Smart dress and more money than sense are prerequisites! (The Casino may move to the Corfu Palace Hotel on Garitsa Bay, Corfu Town.)

APOCALIPSIS Ethnikis Antistasis.
▓ 2300-0300. Ipsos bus from New Fort Bus Station. ● Moderate.
Up-to-the-minute music at this disco in stylish surroundings.

HIPPODROME CLUB Ethnikis Antistasis.
▓ 2300-0300. Ipsos bus from New Fort Bus Station. ● Moderate.
Classy disco with stylish décor and good music.

DANILIA VILLAGE 3 km inland from Gouvia.
▓ 2030-2400 Mon.-Sat. ● Moderate. Good-value inclusive trip with transport, food, wine and entertainment available from many tour operators. *A reconstruction of a Corfiot village, with craft workshops, a museum of folk history and evening floor show. See A-Z.*

KORAKIANA Near Dassia.
▓ 2000-2400. ● Moderate. Good-value inclusive trip with transport, food, wine and entertainment available from many tour operators.
A well-organized venue for Greek dancing, singing and plate-smashing.

EKATH At the junction of Ethnikis Antistasis and the main road.
▓ 2200-0300. Ipsos bus from New Fort Bus Station. ● Moderate.
For a really Greek evening out. This is where the locals go for singing and good bouzouki (see A-Z).

CORFU BY NIGHT Just north of Gouvia on the coast road.
▓ 2130-2400. Bus 7 from San Rocco Square. ● Moderate.
Another genuine Corfiot venue, attracting many Greek performers.

PLANTATION Dassia.
▓ 2300-0300. Bus 7 from San Rocco Square. ● Inexpensive.
On the main road through the town, air-conditioned and popular.

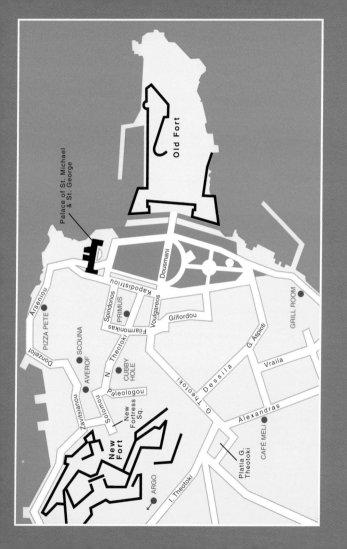

Corfu Town

ARGO Ethnikis Antistasis, New Port.
▨ 1900-0100. ◉ Expensive.
The service is good and the location convenient at the end of a day in town, at this harbourside restaurant specializing in fish and lobster.

GRILL ROOM Corfu Palace Hotel, Garitsa Bay.
▨ 1800-2300. ◉ Expensive.
For good-quality international food in an antiseptic environment.

PRIMUS Panayia Ton Xenon Square, N. Theotoki Street.
▨ 1000-1400, 1730-2330. ◉ Moderate.
White canvas awnings and green chairs are inviting after a hot morning round the town. Drinks and snacks.

PIZZA PETE Arseniou.
▨ 1000-0100. ◉ Moderate.
Perched on the old walls with breezes and views. Pizzas and snacks.

AVEROF Junction of Odhos Alipiou & Prossalendou.
▨ 1100-2400. ◉ Moderate.
Traditional Greek fare at very reasonable prices. In the heart of the Old Town, with some tables outside.

SCOUNA Mitropoleos Square.
▨ 0800-0100. ◉ Moderate.
Traditional fare in a lovely square below the Cathedral. There are tables on both sides of the street, so one or the other should be in the shade.

CAFÉ MELI 30 Alexandras Street.
▨ 1000-1400, 1730-2300. ◉ Inexpensive.
A pastry shop with a small restaurant offering a short but good menu, including delicious pastries and coffee.

CUBBY HOLE Junction of Kotardos & N. Theotoki Street.
▨ 1000-1400, 1700-2300. ◉ Inexpensive.
Small café with delightful shady garden area. Snacks and drinks.

Sidari
Roda
Kassiopi
KALAMI
BEACH
Mount
Pantocrator
PANORAMA
Barbati
Pyrgi
Ipsos
Paleokastritsa
ARIES
Gouvia
MARCO POLO
MANDARIN
PALACE
XENICHTIS
Corfu Town
Ermones
Pelekas
CAFETERIA
KANONI
Sinarades
Benitses
THEODORUS
Moraitika
Messonghi
Lake
Korission
Lefkimmi
Agios
Georgios
Kavos

Island

MANDARIN PALACE On the main road just before Kontokali.
▨ 1200-1600, 1800-0100. Bus 7 from San Rocco Square. ◈ Expensive.
One of several Chinese restaurants on the island, this one has a lovely terrace open to the sea.

XENICHTIS On the airport side of Corfu Town, next to the Polyclinic.
▨ 1900-0200 Mon.-Sat. Bus 4 from San Rocco Square. ◈ Expensive.
Restaurant for a special treat, serving well-presented international dishes.

CAFETERIA KANONI Top of steps to Kanoni Causeway.
▨ 1000-2300. Bus 23 from Esplanade. ◈ Moderate.
Good food, and superb views towards Vlacherna and Pontikonissi.

THEODORUS 2 km south of Benitses.
▨ 1100-1430, 1800-2400. Bus 6 from San Rocco Square. ◈ Moderate.
With a terrace overlooking the bay and shaded by trees, this restaurant specializes in seafood and sometimes has music and dancing.

MARCO POLO Kontokali.
▨ 1100-1500, 1730-2330. Bus 7 from San Rocco Square. ◈ Moderate.
Checked tablecloths, excellent service and good-quality Greek menu.

ARIES Gouvia.
▨ 1100-1430, 1800-2400. Bus 7 from San Rocco Square. ◈ Moderate.
The only really traditional taverna in a sea of chips. Pleasant service and unhurried atmosphere.

PANORAMA Dafnilia Bay.
▨ 1130-1400, 1900-2300. Bus 7 from San Rocco Square, then short walk towards Cape Kommeno (signposted). ◈ Moderate.
Catch the evening sun and gaze across Ipsos Bay to Mount Pantocrator from the large terrace. Wide selection of grills and fish.

KALAMI BEACH Kalami, on the beach.
▨ 0900-2400. Kassiopi bus from New Fort Bus Station. ◈ Moderate.
Simple café looking towards the White House. Excellent Greek salad.

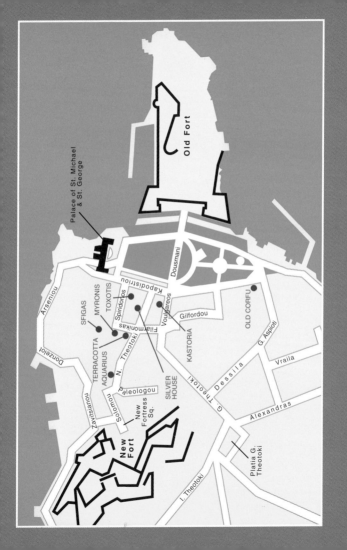

Gifts

SFIGAS 34 Filellinon Street & 16 Filarmonikas Street.
▨ 0930-1330 Mon.-Sat., 1730-2000 Mon.-Fri.
Large selection of gold and silver jewellery in original designs. Helpful English-speaking staff.

TOXOTIS 12 Spiridonos Street & Corfu Palace Hotel.
▨ 0930-2130 Mon.-Sat.
This jewellery shop has an attractive and tempting window display and helpful staff.

AQUARIUS 95 N. Theotoki Street.
▨ 0900-2130 Mon.-Sat.
Pretty jewellery, wall plaques, ceramics and metal sculpture.

SILVER HOUSE 17 N. Theotoki Street.
▨ 1000-1400, 1630-2100 Mon.-Sat.
Modern and Venetian-inspired silver jewellery, candlesticks, dishes and cutlery.

MYRONIS 27 Filarmonikas Street.
▨ 0830-2130.
*Olive wood (see **A-Z**) turned and carved into anything you care to think of, including bowls, breadboards, salad servers and statues.*

TERRACOTTA 2 Filarmonikas Street.
▨ 0900-2300 Mon.-Sat. (summer), 0900-1430, 1730-2030 (winter).
Beautifully displayed handicrafts: ceramics, silk paintings, hand-blown glass, and jewellery.

OLD CORFU 2 Kapodistriou Street.
▨ 1000-1400, 1700-2100.
Exclusive art and antique shop, worth visiting for the artistic display.

KASTORIA 17 Voulgareos Street.
▨ 0900-1300, 1700-2100.
Large selection of fur and leather jackets and coats.

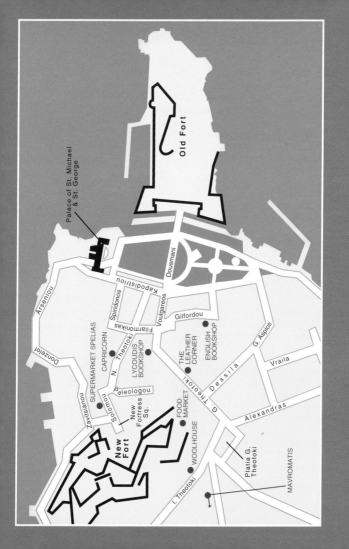

Miscellaneous

WOOLHOUSE 31 I. Theotoki Street (Avramiou).
▦ 0830-1400, 1700-2030.
Articles in pure Greek wool at reasonable prices. All are made on the premises. Orders undertaken.

SUPERMARKET SPELIAS 13 Solomou Street, near the Bus Station. ▦ 0830-1330 Mon.-Sat., 1830-2100 Tue., Thu. & Fri.
Greek and European products in a conveniently situated supermarket.

FOOD MARKET Dessila Street, near the base of the New Fort.
▦ Daily until 1330.
Lively and noisy with colourful displays of fruit and vegetables, fish, cane work, T-shirts, herbs, nuts and tools.

ENGLISH BOOKSHOP 40 Gilfordou Street.
▦ 0900-1330 Mon., Wed., Sat., 0830-1330, 1730-2030 Tue., Thu., Fri.
Books (some antiquarian) in English, French and Italian.

LYCOUDIS BOOKSHOP 65 E. Voulgareos Street.
▦ 0830-1400 Mon. & Wed., 0830-1330 Tue. & Thu.-Sat., 1730-2030 Tue., Thu. & Fri.
Good selection of guidebooks and novels in English.

THE LEATHER CORNER 4 G. Theotoki Street.
▦ 0900-2100 Mon.-Sat.
Large selection of leather bags, clothes, shoes, wallets and belts.

CAPRICORN 67a N. Theotoki Street.
▦ 0930-2130 Mon.-Sat.
Interesting handmade patchwork jackets and kaftans, hand-painted scarves and hand-crocheted shawls.

MAVROMATIS 13 km from Corfu Town on the Paleokastritsa road.
▦ Open mornings only.
Factory shop selling Greek spirits, including ouzo, brandy and koum kouat (see **Drinks***).*

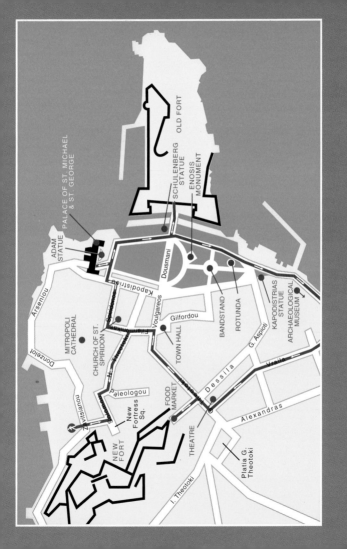

Corfu Town

Duration: 2-3 hr.

Kerkyra, as the town is known locally, is a beautiful blend of many styles, which echo the history of the island. You will see Venetian, British and French influences as well as Greek architecture during the walk, which will give you a flavour of the town.

If you have approached the town by car, park outside the city walls below the New Fort; get there early in order to find a place. If you have come by bus, make your way round the New Fort by way of the harbour road. This is where some of the interisland ferries dock. There are fishing boats and yachts too.

Turn into New Fortress Square, passing neat gardens outside the walls and the winged lions over the Venetian gates to the city. The New Fort (see **ATTRACTIONS 1**) is now open to the public by way of the entrance on Tenedou Street. Return to the square and continue along Solomou Street, keeping right at the end and then forking left into N. Theotoki Street, the heart of the tourist town, with arcaded shops on both sides selling jewellery, leatherwork and clothing.

When the street opens out at a crossroads, turn left down Filarmonikis Street into the Old Town itself. The streets become narrower, steep and stepped, and are paved with polished limestone. Take the first right and you will pass several shops selling candles and icons before you reach the Church of St. Spiridon (see **ATTRACTIONS 1**) on your left. Enter the side door with respect, and you will see the silver casket containing the remains of the island's patron saint behind the altar (see **St. Spiridon**). Leave by the opposite door into Spiridonos Street. Turn right and you will come out on the Esplanade just beside the British-built Palace of St. Michael and St. George (see **ATTRACTIONS 2**), with the famous statue of Adam (see **ATTRACTIONS 2**) outside.

Take a coffee break in one of the cafés of the French-built Listons before crossing the park, passing the cricket ground and fiacre stands (5000 Drs for 30 min), the statue of Schulenberg (see **ATTRACTIONS 1**), and crossing the canal to the Old Fort (see **ATTRACTIONS 1**). Here you can visit the lighthouse and the Chapel of St. George, as well as having fine views of the town from the top.

On leaving the fort, recross the road and turn left down the middle of the park, passing the Enosis monument (marking the union of the island

Kapodistrias Statue

Old Fort

with Greece in 1864), Sir Thomas Maitland's Bandstand (see **ATTRACTIONS 1**) and the Rotunda. Return to the promenade and on your right is the statue of Ioannis Kapodistrias (1776-1831), who campaigned for the union of the Ionian islands with mainland Greece. The promenade drops down from the town here, with a small yacht harbour and anchorage on the left and views across Garitsa Bay to the south. Passing the Corfu Palace Hotel on the right, you will come to a small sign for the Archaeological Museum. Turn right up Vraila Street and after 50 m on the right is the museum entrance (see **ATTRACTIONS 2**), with great terracotta pots outside. The spacious building with its marble floors is wonderfully cool after the heat of the streets.

When you come out, turn right and keep going in as straight a line as possible, passing the telephone exchange, the new theatre and some large and busy government buildings. Cross the main drag of G. Theotoki Street and at the fork turn right. The Food Market (see **SHOPPING 2**) is on your left below the walls of the New Fort. Return to G. Theotoki Street and turn left towards the old bell tower, forking right at the signpost to the Catholic Cathedral. The Venetian-built Town Hall (see **ATTRACTIONS 2**) is on the left as you enter the square, with the Mitropoli Cathedral (see **ATTRACTIONS 2**) at the opposite end. This square is now traffic-free, and there are fountains, flowers, and cafés with umbrellas. Cross Voulgareos Street, behind the Town Hall, and make your way down M. Theotoki Street to N. Theotoki Street, then retrace your steps back to your transport.

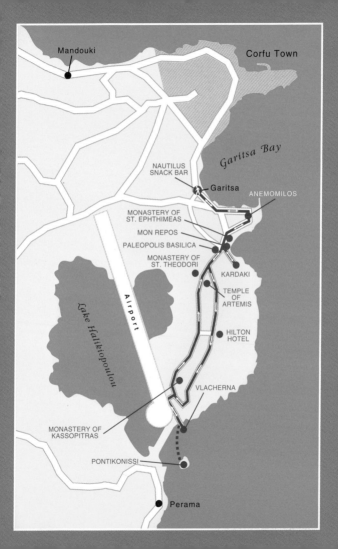

Kanoni

Duration: 2-3 hr.

This walk takes in some of the principal sights of the Kanoni Peninsula to the south of Corfu Town. Either walk or take Bus 2 to Anemomilos from the town, or leave your car along Alkiviadou Dari at the southern end of Garitsa Bay.

Make your way to the Nautilus Snack Bar on the most southerly tip of Garitsa Bay, and follow the road round by the sea. Shortly it turns inland to skirt the Mon Repos Bathing Centre, a shaded area of changing cabins, loungers, cafés and playgrounds mostly used by local people. Keep the high wall on your left and pass several faded villas with overgrown gardens. At the junction turn left into Paleopolis Street, and the Monastery of St. Ephthimeas is on the left (0800-1300, 1700-2000). The gorgeous little whitewashed courtyard is a mass of flowers and cats, and if you are lucky the bell may ring.

Another 100 m will bring you to the quite unmarked but imposing entrance gates of Mon Repos (see **ATTRACTIONS 3**) on your left. The long, winding drive is weedy and overhung with branches of unkempt trees, all grown through with vines and trailing plants. The house, too, has been sadly neglected for many years, the result of a dispute over ownership between King Constantine of Greece and the island of Corfu. But the decaying grandeur has a certain charm, particularly if you manage to be there when no one else is about, even if you cannot see beyond the boarded-up windows and doors. The view from the terrace, too, is obscured by enormous shrubs and mighty cypresses.

As you come out of the gates there are two archaeological sites at the crossroads: the Paleopolis Basilica (see **ATTRACTIONS 3**) on the right and some Roman baths on the left. Turn left along the walls of the grounds of Mon Repos and left again at the end to Kardaki. There are some rather indistinct remains of a temple here, and beyond is the tiny chapel of Agios Marinas, perched on a headland which gives wonderful views back to Corfu Town. Retrace the path to the back of Mon Repos along Analipsis Road, turning left onto Nauskias Road towards Kanoni. This is a one-way street through a residential area with traffic coming towards you, so take care.

After about 1.5 km, walking mostly in the shade of trees, you will come to the Hilton Hotel on the left, and suddenly you are at the end of the

Vlacherna & Pontikonissi

Vlacherna

peninsula, with an improbably picturesque view of the islets of Vlacherna and Pontikonissi (see **ATTRACTIONS 3**). Take a seat at the café and have a cold drink before venturing out to the islands (causeway to Vlacherna, boat to Pontikonissi).

Leave the foreshore by the lower road, which follows the edge of Lake Halikiopoulou. You may see fish traps and wading birds here, but the road veers away between neatly planted market gardens. After some 200 m a track off to the right leads to the little monastery of Kassopitras (0800-1300, 1800-2000). Another 1.5 km will bring you to a main road junction. Turn left past some more delapidated old villas, signposted to Stratia. Keep left at the end of the path and you will see the Monastery of St. Theodori (see **ATTRACTIONS 3**). Opposite are the remains of the Temple of Artemis (see **ATTRACTIONS 3**), dating from the 6thC BC. Return to the main road, keeping left, and you will find yourself back at Mon Repos. Follow the road back towards Anemomilos and the Church of St. Jason and St. Sossipatros (see **ATTRACTIONS 3**), before returning to the Nautilus Snack Bar.

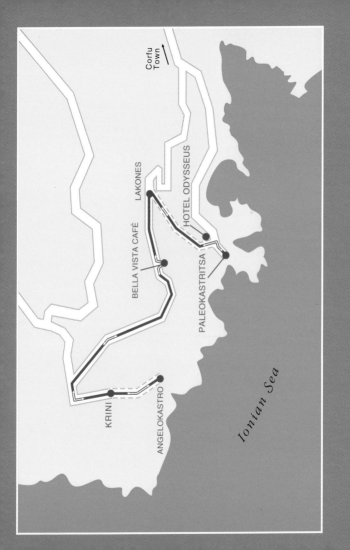

Paleokastritsa & Angelokastro

There is a good road all the way from Corfu Town to Paleokastritsa and regular buses leave from New Fort Bus Station. The first part of the walk is very steep and is only recommended for the fit. Take water with you.

A *Duration: 1 hr each way.*
Leave your car in the free parking area at the bottom of the hill on the left in Paleokastritsa, or get off the bus, and look up the hillside. The little restaurant perching on the cliff edge is your initial goal. Walk back up the road about 300 m and just before the Hotel Odysseus there is a ramp on the left with a blue and white sign reading 'Footpath to Lakones'. Take a deep breath and start to climb. The path winds its way up the hillside past a few houses into the quiet of the olive groves. When you reach the village, which will probably take about 45 min, turn left along the main road. After about 1 km you will reach the Bella Vista Café, where you can recover with a cold drink and admire the fantastic view down this dramatic coast, before continuing along the road to Krini (about 1.5 km) and Angelokastro.

B *Duration: 1 hr each way.*
For those who can do without the climb, take your car to Krini, via Lakones, and park outside the village. There are signs for Angelokastro on the outskirts. Follow these through the village until you reach a gravel path leading through terraced olive groves. As the path begins to descend these suddenly clear to give stunning views of the coast and the castle ruins ahead of you. A slight drop down and a climb back up again will bring you to Angelokastro (see **ATTRACTIONS 4**) itself, which was built in the 13thC and named by Michael Komninos, a strange character from Byzantium who transformed a dark cave into a chapel in honour of the archangels Michael and Gabriel. It is said that signals from here could be seen in Kerkyra (Corfu Town), and it is hard to imagine a more advantageous viewpoint – you can see for miles north and south, across the island and down into the bays of Paleokastritsa.

Achillion Palace: This neoclassical palace was designed by the Italian architect Cardita for Empress Elizabeth of Austria and built in 1891. It was bought by Kaiser Wilhelm II of Germany in 1902 and used as a French military hospital during World War I. It was restored in 1962 by Baron von Richthofen and converted into a casino. It is open to the public but is undergoing renovations to turn it into a conference centre, and the casino has moved to the Hilton Hotel in Kanoni. A few mementos of Elizabeth's time can be seen in the room next to her chapel on the ground floor, and some of the more interesting items include a small statue of Byron and several busts of Greek philosophers. The most impressive piece is a huge bronze of the dying Achilles on the northern terrace, from where there are splendid views to Corfu Town and the mainland. The gardens are extensive and well cared for, but the palace is on the tour bus route and can get crowded. See **ATTRACTIONS 4, EXCURSION 2**.

Archaeological Museum: The outstanding exhibit here is the Gorgon Pediment (see **Gorgons**), discovered in 1911, which dates from the early 6thC BC, when it was part of the Temple of Artemis (see **ATTRACTIONS 3**) in the ancient city of Corcyra. This enormous pediment (17 m wide and 3 m high) depicts a central, fascinatingly hideous figure of Medusa, one of the three Gorgons, with a winged back and serpents writhing on her head and at her waist. She is flanked by her offspring Pegasus and Chrysaor, and guarded by two lion-panthers. The remainder of the frieze is occupied by various mythological figures – gods, goddesses and animals. Almost equally impressive is the beautiful Corinthian statue of a crouching lion (7thC BC), which is said to come from Menecrates' Tomb (see **ATTRACTIONS 3**), and one of the finest animal sculptures of the Classical period. Other exhibits include temple decorations and bronzeware, and a complete set of armour found in a local tomb, which are also worth seeking out. See **ATTRACTIONS 2**.

Bouzouki: This music is at the heart of contemporary Greek culture and for many it represents the essence of Greek music, but the instrument originated in the Orient and was only brought to Greece in 1922 by refugees. It was banned by the authorities at one time and came to represent the resistance movement, and could only be heard in underground clubs and bars. In recent years there has been an upsurge in interest and bouzouki bars are popular contemporary venues for both young and old. See **NIGHTLIFE**.

Church of St. Jason & St. Sossipatros: A very beautiful Byzantine church built in the 12thC and dedicated to two of St. Paul's disciples, who are represented in the church by two fine 16thC icons. They are attributed with bringing Christianity to the island in the 2ndC AD. The intricate terracotta designs on the outer walls have been recognized as Kufic lettering, an early form of Arabic writing often used in this way. The octagonal cupola rests on three ancient monolithic pillars. It is surrounded by a sadly overgrown but shady garden. See **ATTRACTIONS 3**, **WALK 2**.

Church of St. Spiridon: A surprisingly simple and relatively unadorned church (built 1589-96) dedicated to Corfu's much-loved patron saint, St. Spiridon (see **A-Z**), after whom many boys are named (Spiros). The painted ceiling, a 19thC copy of an earlier work, depicts the saint's miracles, and a cluster of 18thC silver hanging lamps and candelabra gleam in the dim light. The gallery also has a fine wrought-iron screen. The mummified body of the saint is kept in a small, dark sanctuary near the altar, which is lit by votive candles and guarded by two priests. The splendid sarcophagus, a gilt casket lavishly embellished with jewels and contained in a silver outer case, is opened and carried upright around Corfu Town four times a year (see **Events**). See **ATTRACTIONS 1**.

Danilia Village: The village was built by the Bouas family as an authentic reconstruction of a typical Corfiot community, in respect of architecture, customs, etc. Among the attractions are St. Irene's Church in the square, a traditional olive press, and a folk museum with displays depicting everyday life in the past. There is also a shopping centre selling Corfiot crafts, and lively evening entertainment with folk dancing and singing, and a set dinner menu, including free wine. See **NIGHTLIFE**.

Town Hall, Corfu Town

Gorgons: In Greek mythology the Gorgons were three sisters –
Medusa, Stheno and Euryale. Medusa had originally been a very
beautiful girl who had dared to compare her looks to those of Athena,
and in punishment Athena turned her hair into snakes and made her
mortal. It was also said that anyone who looked at her would be
turned to stone. Perseus set off to destroy the monster, and by using his
winged sandals to leap into the air and by looking only at the reflec-
tion of Medusa in his shield, he succeeded in cutting off her head.
Pegasus, the winged horse, and the warrior Chrysaor, came to life
from the headless body, and Athena placed the severed head on her
shield so that when they saw it her enemies were turned to stone.

High Commissioners: All the Ionian islands came under British
protection between 1815 and 1864 and there were 10 high commissioners (one of whom was Gladstone). The first two were the most
noteworthy: Sir Thomas Maitland was much disliked by the Corfiots
after he refused to allow Corfu to take part in the War of
Independence against the Turks in 1821 (there is an Ionian-style bandstand named after him on the Spianada – see **ATTRACTIONS 1**); Sir
Frederick Adam was responsible for helping to design a system of
aqueducts to bring water to Corfu Town. These aqueducts are still
functioning today. He was also responsible for building the villa Mon

Repos (see **ATTRACTIONS 3**). There is a statue of Sir Frederick, dressed somewhat incongruously in a toga, in front of the Palace of St. Michael and St. George (see **ATTRACTIONS 2**).

Ithaca: One of the smallest of the Ionian islands, approximately 29 km by 6 km, with a population of about 6500, one-third of whom live in the capital Ithaca Town (or Vathi), Ithaca has considerable traditional character, extremely helpful and friendly residents, and is still relatively unspoilt by tourism. The island is separated from its larger neighbour Kephalonia by a wide channel, and the ferry service to Ithaca is connected with that to Kephalonia. Roads on the island can be very rough but there is a bus service and taxis are available. The main ferry terminus is at Ithaca Town on the east coast, the town's dazzling white houses clinging to the hillside which overlooks the deep U-shaped Bay of Molos.

This mountainous yet lush island is reputedly the birthplace of Odysseus and it is said that he hid the gifts given to him by the Phaeacians in the Cave of the Nymphs or Marble Cave, 3 km north of Ithaca Town. Further north is Kathara Monastery, built 600 m above sea level, with outstanding views from the bell tower. Stavros, 19 km northwest of Ithaca Town, is a friendly, rural village with taverna accommodation, and is an excellent starting point from which to explore the north of the island, including the Bay of Polis (20 min walk towards the coast from Stavros), with its tiny quay, colourful local fishing boats and legendary sunken city. Nearby is another cave, Loizos Cave, where archaeologists discovered fragments of pottery indicating the worship of Artemis, Hera and Athena. Pelikata, 1 km north of Stavros, is the site of another excavation which confirmed the existence of a Bronze-Age settlement (from 2200 BC) and strengthens the claim that the ancient city of Ithaca was built in the area. Frikes and Kioni (16 km and 20 km northeast of Ithaca Town) are both peaceful, unassuming and typically Ionian seaside villages.

A trip to this little island is well worth considering and a day trip could be included in a visit to Kephalonia. Accommodation is scarce but there are a few hotels, and some rooms are available in tavernas and private houses. See **ISLANDS**.

Kassiopi: Despite recent developments as a tourist resort, this friendly seaside village still retains considerable character and individuality, as well it might, considering its past importance as a flourishing port visited by such eminent people as Cicero, Cato and Nero, who reputedly gave one of his last recitals here. The 13thC hillside fortress, now ruined, is a reminder of Kassiopi's past significance and is well worth a visit, as is the Panagia Kassiotropi Church with its 17thC frescoes. To the north of Kassiopi are unspoilt beaches of white sand and pebbles. See **ATTRACTIONS 4, BEACHES 1, EXCURSION 1**.

Kephalonia: Mountainous and majestic, the largest of the Ionian islands looms dramatically and unforgettably out of the sea. This 737 km² island is home to 31,000 inhabitants, most of whom live around the main town, Argostolion, 23 km west of Sami, the ferry terminus and usual point of arrival. Sami has little to recommend it, but do try to see the Roman remains with frescoes just outside the town. West of Sami are the underground sea caves of Mellissani and Drogorati (the Fiscardo bus will take you within a short walk of the caves, or it's a 30 min drive). Agia Efimia (10 km north of Sami) is a delightful fishing port with good restaurants.

A severe earthquake in 1953 virtually destroyed the old town of Argostolion (west of Sami), founded by the Venetians in 1757, which has been rebuilt on a rather unimaginative grid pattern. There is an archaeological museum (mainly Mycenaean artefacts), a folk museum, and a cathedral with beautiful icons. The famous Katavrothes (swallow holes) are just 2.5 km from Argostolion and are a rare geological phenomenon where the sea seems to disappear undergound. In fact, it crosses under the island and reappears at Melissani, where it once emerged with such a powerful force that it was used to operate two mills.

There are a number of interesting sites accessible from Argostolion. Kastro (5 km), the former island capital, was destroyed by an earthquake in 1636; its Greek and Venetian buildings lie in ruins on a hillside crowned by a castle. Lord Byron once stayed in Metaxata (9 km), where you will find some Mycenaean tombs and a ruined temple. Lakithra (10 km) also has some Mycenaean tombs and is the richest, most fertile area in the region. Maxacarata (18 km) has a necropolis with several Mycenaean tombs. The Castle of St. George (25 km, near Peratata), built by the Venetians in 1504, is very atmospheric, with sweeping views. Just beneath it is Agios Andreos Monastery with its outstanding collection of icons. North of Argostolion is Lixourion, a peaceful, old-fashioned town where you will find vestiges of the ancient city of Pali, and a folk museum in an old mansion. There are good beaches to the south. The late-16thC castle in the delightful village of Assos (67 km north of Lixourion) was built by the Venetians to protect the inhabitants from pirate raids. Fiscardo (56 km north of Assos) is a quiet 12thC fishing port looking across to Ithaca, protected by a dense forest of cypress trees. Kephalonia will amply reward a stay of three days. There are hotels in Argostolion, Sami and Poros. Buses operate throughout the island. Motorcycle and scooter hire tends to be expensive as only larger engines can tackle the terrain. See **ISLANDS**.

Lefkada: With its densely covered mountainsides, vast golden beaches and picturesque villages, Lefkada (32 km by 12 km; population 25,000) must be everyone's idea of a typical Greek island. Access is by bus from Athens (across the bridge which spans the narrow channel separating Lefkada from the mainland) or by boat from Kephalonia, Kioni and Ithaca. Lefkada Town (population 6500) is small and picturesque, and situated in the north of the island on a natural harbour overlooking a huge lagoon. Note the brightly coloured wooden houses and be sure to visit the Castle of Santa Maura, founded in 1300 by John Orsini, a Frankish knight. Two churches are worth seeing: Agios Dimitrios has four paintings by Panaghiotis Doxaras, and Agios Minas has ceiling paintings by Nicolas Doxaras. An archaeological museum at 21 Phaneromenis Street displays finds from the Bronze Age to Roman times.

Interesting trips from Lefkada Town might include the ruins of Old Lefkada (polygonal enclosure, theatre and acropolis) 3 km away on the Nidri road, and Nidri, 18 km south of Lefkada Town on the east coast, a popular holiday resort and fishing port, and erstwhile home (now a museum) of the German archaeologist Dorpfeld, who claimed

that Lefkada was Homer's Ithaca. Look across from here to the islets of
Scorpio, Scorpios, Sparti and Madouri. There is a good shingle bathing
beach at peaceful Poros, 11 km south of Nidri. Wander along the village's narrow, winding lanes and explore the old church with its 17thC
paintings of the Virgin. Frescoes from the 15thC adorn the Church of
Agios Georgios de Bisa at Marandochori, 33 km from Lefkada Town.
The fishing village of Vassiliki, 40 km from Lefkada Town, has a pleasant, shady quay and extensive shingle beach, and boat trips leave
from here to several small islands. The lighthouse at Lefkata, 58 km
from Lefkada Town, stands on the site of the once world-famous shrine
to Apollo, and here, too, it is said that Sappho, rejected by her
beloved Phaona, leapt to her death from the cliffs. For a glimpse of traditional rural island life, visit the village of Karia, 76 km from Lefkada
Town, and stroll along its twisting, crowded lanes, enjoying the pretty
gardens. There are many picturesque country walks that will take you
to the heart of the island.

You should allow 2-3 days to enjoy the whole of Lefkada.
Accommodation available on the island ranges from hotels to camp
sites. Transport includes buses and taxis, as well as moped and scooter
hire. See **ISLANDS**.

Monastery of Platitera: An enchanting 17thC monastery north-west of Corfu Town, set in a small white courtyard with pink stone walls. The lofty bell tower is Venetian but the buildings are traditional Greek style. Be sure to visit the church and see the finely carved wooden screen, and the icon of the Virgin Mary which was presented by Count John Capodistrias, first president of independent Greece (1827-31), whose tomb can also be found here. There are some well-preserved examples of the Cretan school of painting at the rear of the church. See **ATTRACTIONS 3**.

Museum of Asiatic Art: Normally housed in the Palace of St. Michael and St. George, which is currently (1993) closed for renovation, the collection comprises more than 10,000 pieces of Oriental art dating from Neolithic times to the 19thC. It was formed by Gregory Manos, a Greek diplomat and scholar who offered the collection to the state in 1917 and died, relatively impoverished, 11 years later. The Manos collection was augmented by another diplomat, Nickolaos Hadzivasileion, who donated bronzes, screens and sculptures from Nepal, Tibet, India, Thailand, Korea and Japan. The main collection ranges from Chinese pottery and porcelain from ancient to modern times, to tomb figures and bronzes, and a Japanese collection with books, prints, masks and weapons. See **ATTRACTIONS 2**.

Natural History:
Vegetation: 3.5 million olive trees produce Corfu's main crop and yield olives every second year from early Nov. to the following spring (see **Olive Wood**). The cypress, the second most common tree, is a conifer with exceptionally hard wood and dense dark foliage, and contrasts strongly with the olive, an evergreen with narrow leaves. The vine is not extensively cultivated, and although most fruits grow readily, only the orange and lemon are commercially produced. Wide areas of the island are completely overgrown by kermes oak, myrtle, arbutus, lentisk and a profusion of aromatic plants. Lawrence Durrell's *Prospero's Cell* and Gerald Durrell's *My Family and Other Animals* contain vivid descriptions of the Corfu countryside.
Wildlife: Mammals resident include foxes, jackals, weasels, moles,

hedgehogs, dormice and hares. Reptiles include tortoises, frogs, toads, lizards and snakes (mostly harmless). There is a wide variety of birdlife, including some rare species of white barn owl, and herons and king-fishers can occasionally be seen (see **Bird-watching**).

Flowers: The anemone appears in mid-Jan. and by Feb. or Mar. Corfu's stunning display is well under way. By the time the Judas trees blossom in May the show is in full swing and lasts until the end of June. The last flower of the year is the snowdrop in Nov. Corfu's heavier rainfall means that flowers, both wild and cultivated, grow abundantly and the scent from the flowering trees – wisteria, myrtle, oleander, lemon and orange – is sometimes almost overpowering.

Old Fort: Built by the Venetians in 1550, although some sections dating from a much earlier period already existed, this formidable structure stands on two levels to the east of Corfu Town, and is separated from it by an artificial moat, giving it an ideal defensive position. In fact, the town's entire population lived within its walls from the 6th to the 13thC. Today its architectural features reflect the British occupation during Victoria's reign. It served as a military hospital from 1836 to 1864 and again in World War I. Now a military academy, the fort is open to the public but photography is not allowed. Once the present (1993) renovations are finished, it will again serve as an open-air theatre in summer for a sound-and-light show and cultural events. See **ATTRACTIONS 1**.

Olive Wood: Turning and carving olive wood is one of Corfu's traditional crafts. The grain in this slow-growing wood is convoluted and intricate, twisting and turning with the trunk of these venerable trees. The wood must be stored and dried out slowly for at least four years before it can be worked without splitting. It makes particularly beautiful salad servers and bowls. See **SHOPPING 1**, **Natural History**.

Palace of St. Michael & St. George: Royal Palace. This fine Classical-style, colonnaded building on the northern side of the Esplanade was constructed between 1819 and 1823 with stone shipped from Malta, and was intended as a residence for the British Lord High

Commissioners (see **A-Z**). The frieze on the façade represents the emblems of the Ionian islands. The rooms are airy and spacious with superb marble fireplaces, and those in the western wing have glorious sea views. There is a particularly handsome staircase in the entrance hall. The staterooms are normally open to visitors but the palace is currently undergoing restoration (1993). See **ATTRACTIONS 2**, **WALK 1**.

Paleokastritsa: It is no wonder that Paleokastritsa is the best-known resort on Corfu. The six small coves are washed by unbelievably clear blue water which is a paradise for divers. Backed by sand and pebble beaches, dramatic cliffs and sea caverns, with tree-covered hills sweeping down to the bay, the setting is hard to beat. It does get very busy at the height of the season, but a short boat trip to one of the more inaccessible coves is rewarding. The road from Corfu Town was constructed by British army engineers 150 years ago and is still one of the best on the island. It is well used daily by tourists in buses, on mopeds, in hire cars and on organized tours. The 13thC Byzantine monastery (see **ATTRACTIONS 4**) perched on the promontory above the resort is well worth a visit for its tranquil atmosphere and wonderful views. Its strategic position gave the monastery military significance – note the early-18thC Russian cannon outside – and later it was used by the British as a convalescent hospital for soldiers. Offshore, the famous Kolouri Rock is said to be the ship which took Odysseus home to Ithaca after his wanderings, petrified by the angry sea-god Poseidon. From the village of Lakones above the resort you will get a bird's-eye view of the dramatic coastline, Paleokastritsa itself and the ruins of cliff-top Angelokastro (see **WALK 3**). See **BEACHES 2**, **EXCURSION 2**.

Paxos: The smallest of the main Ionian islands (10 km by 4 km), with a population of 2500, Paxos is covered with olive trees, many extremely large and old, twisted and bent into extraordinary shapes. Exceptionally clear water is irresistible to divers and snorkellers, and although beaches are mainly shingle, there are plenty of flat rocks for diving and coves for sunbathing. Gaios, the main town and port, is a pleasant little community with some gracious 19thC houses and a small white church. Bicycles and mopeds are on hire and the roads are quiet if a little rough. There is good bathing at the pretty northern village of Laka, which lies in a sheltered bay. The low-built houses are painted in various shades of brown and blue and you may be lucky enough to hear the particularly beautiful Russian bells ring out from the Byzantine church. The west coast is very steep with several interesting sea caves, including the Seven Seas Caves and the Grotto of Ypapanti (Poseidon's Cave), the towering Ortholithos Rock and the white Mousmouli Cliffs. There is little shelter along this coast so it is advisable to take an organized boat trip from Gaios or Laka. Other excursion destinations include the delightful Antipaxos, a tiny satellite island to the south with gorgeous beaches, a taverna or two, and very limited accommodation, and Mogonissi, another tiny islet off Gaios, which has a restaurant, sandy beach, camp site and cool sea breezes. Panayia off the east coast has thermal springs and a shrine to the Virgin Mary which attracts pilgrims. The feast of the Assumption is celebrated on 15 Aug. in the main square of Gaios.

There is a limited amount of accommodation on Paxos but there are apartments and villas which can be prebooked. Private rooms and houses are available; ask round in Gaios, though people will meet the ferry offering rooms. Camping is restricted to recognized sites because of the danger of fire. If the overcommercialization of Corfu gets you down, this is the place to escape to. Nightlife is minimal, restaurants are traditional, and a Greek island is alive and well. See **ISLANDS**.

Royal Palace: See **Palace of St. Michael & St. George**.

St. Spiridon: Born in Cyprus in the 4thC AD, Spiridon was a shepherd before becoming a monk and then a bishop. He was renowned for his piety and the performance of some minor miracles. He died in AD 350 and his body was taken to Constantinople, but was later hurriedly removed, wrapped in a straw basket tied to the back of a donkey, before the Turks overran the city in the 15thC. He is much loved by the Corfiots. See **Church of St. Spiridon**, **Events**.

Town Hall: A fine example of 17thC Venetian architecture, the building became a theatre in 1720 and now houses the offices of Corfu Town's administrators. There is a bust of Doge Francesco Morosini, the military leader who defeated the Turks in the Peloponnese War of 1684-7, on the external east wall. See **ATTRACTIONS 2**.

Zakinthos: The island is about 27 km by 38 km, with a population of approximately 30,000, of whom almost one-third live in Zakinthos Town. Strangely reminiscent of England with its country lanes and lush, green fields divided by hedges, Zakinthos is one of the least spoilt and tourist-orientated of the Ionian islands.

Zakinthos Town, the island's capital, was largely reconstructed after the 1953 earthquake and retains its old-world atmosphere, although few genuinely old buildings remain. See the ruins of the Old Fortress on the hill behind the town and the Church of Agios Dionysus (3 km towards Argassi beach). The town museum has a collection of 16th-19thC icons and some post-Byzantine wall paintings (0830-1445 Mon., Wed. & Sat., 0800-1300 Sun.). The poets Solomos and Calvos were born in Zakinthos and there is a museum dedicated to them in Agios Moikos Square.

The roads on Zakinthos are in fairly good condition and there is a re-liable bus service. Macherados (13.5 km on the Laganas road) has two 14thC churches, one half-ruined and the other, Agia Mavra, with a splendid interior and a beautiful icon. Enjoy the exceptional views of the island from the scrub-covered plateau at Agios Nicolas (27 km from Zakinthos Town, near the west coast), and travel further north to Volimes, a large town with a Venetian tower and 12th-14thC frescoes. The magical Blue Caves, where the play of light on the water refracted and reflected a thousand times creates a spellbinding show of colour, are at the northernmost tip of the island, accessible by road from Volimes or by boat from St. Nicholas Bay. A rather different experience awaits visitors to Xyngia Cave (on the northeast coast) as it shelters a sul-phurous spring. Laganas (on the south coast) is the island's only true resort and has a fine, sandy beach with unusual rock formations, while Keri, on the south peninsula, is a sleepy, friendly village at the foot of the hills. The 17thC church here is worth a look and there are some strange pitch (or tar) springs in the bay.

Allow two days for a visit to the island. There are hotels, and rooms in private houses. Access is by ferry from Killini on the Greek mainland (connections with Athens) or by air. See **ISLANDS**.

Corfu Town Harbour

Accidents & Breakdowns: In the event of an accident with another vehicle, follow the usual procedure of exchanging names, addresses and insurance details. If you are driving a hire car, contact the hire company immediately; they usually speak good English and will advise you what to do. The police are reluctant to intervene unless someone has been injured. The most common accidents involve inexperienced holiday-makers on mopeds. There are agents for most of the common makes of car in Corfu Town who can assist with breakdowns, and local mechanics can be helpful, efficient and reasonable. See **Consulates**, **Driving**, **Emergency Numbers**.

Accommodation: There are six official categories of hotel, ranging from the luxurious to the very basic (Lux, A-E). The best value for money is often found in the C and D family-run rooms. In high season it can be difficult to find hotel accommodation unless you have pre-booked. Travel agents and the NTOG (National Tourist Office of Greece) have lists of hotels, and the tourist police, tel: 30265, can be helpful. There is no accommodation service at the port or at the airport.
Rooms & tavernas (C, D & E): No advance booking. At the port and airport people will offer rooms. Alternatively, get the bus to the area of your choice and ask. Expect to pay around 5000 Drs a night.
Private villas & apartments (A & B): Self-catering accommodation is let by the week. Prebooking is usually necessary but again it is worth asking locally. Expect to pay the equivalent of 10,000-15,000 Drs a night.
Hotels (Lux, A & B): Prebooking essential. Expect to pay up to 20,000 Drs a night at the best hotels. With accommodation exceeding demand, it is worth asking at the complexes used by package holiday operators if there are any rooms free, with prices around 10,000-15,000 Drs.
Breakfast is not always included in the price, and you may get a reduction for a stay of more than two nights. See **Camping**, **Tourist Information**, **Youth Hostels**.

Airport: The airport is 2 km southwest of Corfu Town and handles domestic (within Greece) and international flights. Tel: 30180 for information. There is no tourist office at the airport but there are shops, a bar, a cafeteria, toilets and exchange facilities, and car hire desks. There is a taxi rank outside (around 2000 Drs into Corfu Town) but make sure you agree a price before you set off. There are hotel shuttle buses but the nearest public bus is on the main road, a 500 m walk away. It is about a 30 min walk into the centre of Corfu Town.

Antiques: The export of antique icons and any other objects of historical interest, found in the sea or elsewhere, is strictly prohibited.

Baby-sitters: There are no agencies or approved lists of locally available baby-sitters, but ask at your hotel reception. The Greeks are very fond of children and someone will probably be happy to listen out for them. See **Children**.

Banks: See **Currency**, **Money**, **Opening Times**.

Barbecues: Barbecues are becoming increasingly popular and are organized by tour operators, hotels and tavernas. The more elaborate may take place on beaches that can only be reached by boat and may take all day. Departing at around 1000, with lunch included in the trip, and returning at 1600, prices are around 4500 Drs per person and are generally good value.

Beaches: The Corfu authorities have done a commendable job in cleaning up the waters around the coast. Bathing is even possible around Corfu Town these days, though it is not particularly recommended as there are so many more attractive places nearby. Many of the east coast resorts have rather narrow shingle beaches; if you want softer sand head for the northwest to Sidari, Roda or Agios Stefanos. In many places you can catch a boat to the more inaccessible and less crowded coves. Nude sunbathing is prohibited, but topless bathing is tolerated and widespread. However, use your discretion and do not offend by stripping off on town beaches. See **BEACHES 1 & 2**.

Best Buys: The Organization of Corfiot Cultural Activities (OKE) actively encourages folk art and craft, and visitors are usually welcome

to watch craftsmen and -women at work. Pottery, leather work, weaving of wall hangings and rugs, turning and carving of olive wood (see **A-Z**), metalwork (including silver, copper, gold and wrought iron), crochet and lacemaking are crafts which are all thriving throughout the island. Jewellery is a particularly good buy on Corfu, with designs showing Minoan, Mycenaean, Macedonian and Venetian influences. The main shopping area in Corfu Town stretches from The Listons through the Old Town to New Fortress Square. See **SHOPPING 1 & 2**, **Markets**, **Shopping**.

Bicycle & Motorcycle Hire: Bicycles are widely available on Corfu and the charge is around 1500 Drs a day for a mountain bike. But remember that the roads are often full of potholes and the heat can make cycling exhausting. If you do cycle, always take water with you. Corfu is quite hilly too, and mountainous in the north. Motorcycles of all sizes are available for hire and are an ideal way of getting about if you know what you are doing.

You will need to be over 18 and have a full driving licence. Insurance is usually included in the charge but make sure it is, as accidents on these machines are all too common as a result of inexperience, poor road conditions and overloading. The wearing of a helmet is actually a legal requirement so not wearing it may invalidate your insurance. Prices vary from 3500 Drs per day for a 50 cc moped, 4000 Drs per day for a scooter and 7000 Drs per day for a scrambler to 9000 Drs per day for a Harley-Davidson lookalike.

Bird-watching: During the spring and autumn migrations many birds from northern Europe rest here on their way south. Unfortunately, this is as far as many of them get, for shooting small birds is a habit the locals are finding it hard to break. The lakes of Korission in the southwest and Halikiopoulou by the airport attract waders and ducks, heron and egrets. Golden orioles and hoopoes are fairly common.

Budget: 1993 prices. Typical prices are given below but these will be higher in up-market establishments such as those in The Listons, in luxury hotels and at tourist traps.

Hotel breakfast	800 Drs
Restaurant lunch	2000 Drs
Coffee (instant)	250 Drs
Beer	300 Drs
Soft drink	250 Drs
Greek brandy	500 Drs

Buses: There are two bus services, both of which have a much increased frequency in the summer months:

City Buses are blue and run from the terminal at San Rocco Square (0700-2130), and include services to Achillion (Bus 7); Benitses (Bus 6); Dassia (Bus 7); and Pelekas (Bus 11). Bus 2 to Kanoni leaves from the Esplanade. Buses get very crowded and timetables are flexible to say the least. Expect to pay 140 Drs to Gouvia and 200 Drs to Benitses.

Long-distance buses (KTEL) are green and cream and leave from the New Fort Bus Station to the east of the New Fort, between the New Port and San Rocco Square. A timetable is available from the tourist office or the bus station. There are regular departures for Kavos (600 Drs), Paleokastritsa (320 Drs), Kassiopi (460 Drs), Sidari (460 Drs) and Ipsos (220 Drs), as well as to the larger of the west coast beaches such as Agios Georgios (420 Drs), Agios Gordios (220 Drs) and Agios Stefanos (460 Drs). The last bus service is around 1900.

Bus services to the mainland from New Fort Bus Station operate at 0845 daily, reaching Athens at 1815; via Kavos on Mon., Wed. and Fri., departing at 0645; and to Thessalonika at 0700 daily and 1815 Thu. and Sun. Prices start at 6150 Drs.

Cameras & Photography: Most makes of film, batteries, video tapes and accessories are available in Corfu Town but they can be expensive. Films and batteries may be obtainable in supermarkets around the island but not video accessories. Film processing is widely available but the quality varies. A charge is made for photography in some places, e.g. the Archaeological Museum. Use your discretion when photographing local people – always ask and smile.

Camping: There are 14 official camp sites with the usual facilities. Average prices are 400 Drs per person per day; 500 Drs for a tent. Unauthorized camping is not allowed.
Kontokali Beach International, Kontokali, tel: 91202; Dionissos Camping, Kommeno, tel: 91417; Karda Beach, Dassia, tel: 93595; Ipsos Ideal Camping, Ipsos, tel: 93243; Corfu Camping, Ipsos, tel: 93579; Paradise, Pyrgi, tel: 93558; Paleokastritsa, tel: 0663-41204; Sea Horse, Messonghi, tel: 55364; Vatos Pelekas, Vatos, tel: 94505; Cormarie, Korakiana, tel: 93587; San Georgio, Kavadades, tel: 0663-51194; Karousades Camping, Karousades, tel: 0663-31415; Roda Beach Camping, Roda, tel: 0663-93120; Dolphin, Sidari, tel: 0663-31253.

Car Hire: Most international car hire companies operate on the island alongside local operators. Charges are not unduly high – around 60,000 Drs a week for the smallest car – and credit cards are widely accepted. You will need to present your British driving licence and some companies ask for an international licence. Some may refuse drivers under 25. Check the insurance cover you are offered.
Holiday Autos, 128 I. Theotoki Street, tel: 28029; International Rent a Car, 20 Kapodistriou Street, tel: 37710/33411; Inter-Corfu Rent-a-Moto, Ipsos, tel: 93607/43960/93756; Euro-Hire, 132 I. Theotoki Street, tel: 22062/34575/28143.
See **Driving**.

Chemists: Look for the sign with a red cross on a white background. Prescriptions are needed for treatments for stomach problems and for sleeping pills. See **Health**, **Opening Times**.

Children: The Greeks are very fond of children and they are accepted (and welcome) in most establishments. There are two recreation parks in Corfu Town with swings, slides, roundabouts and climbing frames. The best is opposite the cricket pitch, next to the Old Fort; the other, at Garitsa on the Kanoni road, is not so well kept. Most resorts and hotel complexes offer organized activities for children. If a child is lost, contact the tourist police, tel: 30265, or the local village police, but remember that the latter may speak little or no English. See **Baby-sitters**.

Climate: It is not always sunny in Corfu. More rain falls here than on the Greek mainland and in spring it can be quite wet. By May, however, it is warm, with plenty of sunshine (19°C-24°C). June-Sep. is hot and dry (18°C-35°C), but cool sea breezes allow comfortable nights. Autumn brings occasional thunderstorms but generally good weather (16°C-22°C) and winters are rainy and cool (5°C-12°C), although snow is practically unknown.

Complaints: If you have any complaints about service or the quality of food, make your first representations to the manager of the hotel or restaurant concerned. Tour operators and representatives are helpful with problems over accommodation or the organization of your holiday. The tourist police, tel: 30265, have some authority when it comes to overcharging, for example with taxis. The tourist office is also willing to listen.

Consulates:
UK – 1 Menekratos, Corfu Town, tel: 37995/30055.
Consulates for the Republic of Ireland, Australia, Canada, New Zealand and the USA are in Athens.

Conversion Chart:

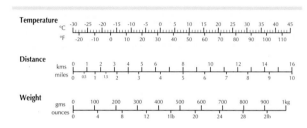

Credit Cards: See **Money**.

Crime & Theft: There is very little crime on the island but you should always keep your valuables in the hotel safe. If something is stolen, inform your tour operator, the hotel manager and the police (see **A-Z**). You may need a certificate from the police to claim on your insurance (see **A-Z**). See **Consulates**, **Emergency Numbers**.

Culture:
Customs & traditions: The Organization of Corfiot Cultural Activities (OKE), 5 Manzaro Street, tel: 32685, has revived many customs, such as the Varcarola and the Carnival.
Music: Corfu Town supports three philharmonic orchestras and choirs which also perform abroad. There are eleven others around the island.
Singing & dancing: The Kerkyra Choir, the Kerkyraiki Kandata, Kerkyraiki Mantolinata, Laodamas and Lykio Ellinidon give regular performances at the Kerkyraiko Chorogramma and the Municipal Theatre in Corfu Town. The Corfu Dance Workshop are a popular contemporary group.

Theatre: The Kerkyraiki Kallitechniki Skini theatre group travels around the island performing, as well as appearing at the Municipal Theatre in Corfu Town.
See **Events**.

Currency: The drachma (Dr) is the Greek monetary unit.
Coins – 5, 10, 20, 50, 100 Drs.
Notes – 50, 100, 500, 1000, 5000 Drs.
See **Money**.

Customs Allowances:

UK/EC	Cigarettes	Cigarillos	Cigars	Tobacco	Still Table Wine	Spirits/Liqueurs	Fortified Wine	Additional Still Table Wine	Perfume	Toilet Water	Gifts & Souvenirs
Duty Free	*or* 200	*or* 100	*or* 50	250g	2 *l*	*or* 1 *l*	*or* 2 *l*	2 *l*	60 cc/ml	250 cc/ml	£32
Duty Paid	800	400	200	1kg	90 *l*	10 *l*	20 *l*				

With the Single European Market, travellers are subject only to highly selective spot checks. The red and green channels no longer apply within the EC. There is no restriction, either by quantity or value, on *duty-paid* goods purchased in another country, provided they are for the purchaser's *own personal use* (guidelines have been published). If you are unsure of certain items, check with the customs officials as to whether payment of duty is required.

Disabled People: There are very few facilities for the disabled and wheelchairs are something of a novelty, causing people to stare. There are no designated parking areas or wheelchair ramps, roads are extremely uneven and kerbs can be high, but restaurant, shop and hotel staff are all helpful. Make sure you choose a hotel with ground-floor facilities or a lift – these are not common. See **Health**.

Drinks:

Wines: The island does not produce any commercially available wines, though you will find a rough home-brew available in village tavernas. The best-known wine is retsina, a white wine flavoured with pine resin and best drunk ice-cold. It is the perfect accompaniment to the olive oil-rich Greek cooking and is very reasonable at 500 Drs for half a litre. There are plenty of good-quality wines available from the Greek mainland and you will find imported wine in the most expensive restaurants.

Apéritif: Ouzo is an aniseed-flavoured spirit which turns milky when water is added. Drink this cold with a dish of tzatziki or taramasalata.

Spirits: Metaxa, Botrys and Cambas are the three most famous Greek brandies and they are all available in 3-star, 5-star and vintage versions. Raki is a fearsome spirit distilled from the grape skins left over after wine-making. It is served in tiny glasses and should be thrown down the throat in one go – but sipping is probably safer. *Koum kouat* is another vicious spirit which is brewed exclusively on the island and is drunk at the end of a meal.

Beer: Lager beers are very popular and inexpensive. Amstel is brewed under licence in Greece and is widely available. Fix and Hellas are similar Greek brews.

Water: Tap water is mostly desalinated sea water and unpalatable. Corfu bottled water is available everywhere and costs 60-90 Drs a litre.

Driving: It is necessary to have a UK, EC or international driving licence and third-party insurance. Drive on the right, overtake on the left, and give priority to traffic from the right unless otherwise indicated. The use of horns in towns is theoretically prohibited and the use of seat belts is compulsory – failing to wear one may invalidate your insurance. The Greek Automobile and Touring Club (ELPA), tel: 104, provides a free service to members of foreign auto clubs such as the AA and the RAC. Avoid the centre of Corfu Town where the narrow streets are congested and parking impossible. Otherwise, the roads are reasonable,

though even the best are liable to have potholes and unstable edges. Do not venture onto unsurfaced roads which are marked on better maps. Signposts are mostly bilingual Greek/English but hazard-warning signs are few and far between, e.g. for hairpin bends. In more remote areas you will find goats, sheep, chickens, dogs and heavily-laden donkeys with their owners on the road, so drive carefully. See **Accidents & Breakdowns**, **Parking**, **Petrol**.

Drugs: Drugs are not tolerated. Possession of small quantities can result in imprisonment and a fine. Trafficking can mean life imprisonment.

Eating Out: Eating out is half the fun of a holiday and Corfu offers a wide range of possibilities. The bakers, market and supermarkets provide a wealth of ingredients for picnics and self-caterers; there are takeaways which vary from souvlakia bars selling a portable meal of barbecued meat and salad in pitta bread to pizzerias and hamburger joints; for a traditional Greek meal, head for a taverna; for a celebration there are more expensive restaurants offering international cuisine. Lunch is generally served 1200-1500 and the evening meal 1800-late. In the more traditional restaurants you will be invited into the kitchen to see the dish of the day or to choose your fish. The menu will show two prices, with and without tax. You pay the inclusive price along with a cover charge which includes bread and service. You may tip as well if the service and food have pleased you. There are so many places to eat that you will be spoilt for choice, but don't be put off looking at menus by pushy proprietors – competition is fierce and touting common. See **RESTAURANTS 1 & 2**, **Food**.

Electricity: 220 V. Two-pin plugs are used; adaptors are available in most electrical retailers.

Emergency Numbers:

Police	100
Ambulance	45811 (5 lines)
Fire	199
Tourist police	30265

Events:

January: The traffic police receive gifts from motorists, and children also receive presents; *6:* Epiphany, Blessing of the Waters, children dive into the bay in front of the Nautical Club to look for a cross previously blessed by the bishop.

February: Two-week Carnival with masked balls and dressing up for the children, who hit each other with plastic batons.

Mardi Gras Sunday: Parade in Corfu Town with fancy dress and huge floats. In Episkepsis the priests dance slowly and solemnly through the village to the sound of chanting.

Clean Monday: The first day of Lent, usually celebrated by family picnic outings.

Good Friday: Decorated bier with representation of Christ's body carried in a silent procession through the streets.

Easter Sunday: At 1100 residents throw a piece of pottery out of their windows. This strange custom is peculiar to Corfu and is thought to symbolize the casting out of Judas. In the evening the bishop celebrates Mass on the Spianada and at 2400 church bells ring, firework shows begin and everyone lights a candle.

1 May: Families make for the coast to picnic in cars brightly decorated with flowers; *21:* Union Day, marking the union of the Ionian islands with Greece when the British left on 21 May 1864, with a parade and cannon, and a performance by the Corfu Town Philharmonic Orchestra near The Listons.

28 October: Soldiers and schoolchildren parade to commemorate the rejection of Mussolini's ultimatum in 1940, which then involved Greece in World War II.

12 December: St. Spiridon's feast day. All males named Spiridon receive a gift and the saint's body is exposed for three days so that devotees may kiss its velvet slipper.

St. Spiridon processions: These commemorate the miracles performed by the saint (see **A-Z**) and take place on 11 Aug. (saved the island from the Turks), 1st Sun. in Nov. and Palm Sunday (saved the island twice from plague), and Sat. of Holy Week (saved the island from famine). There are colourful processions through the streets, following the saint's relics in a gilt casket (see **Church of St. Spiridon**).

Village saints' days or Panighiri: Churches are specially decorated, lambs are roasted on spits in the street, bands play, and in the evening a parade of local dignitaries, churchmen and school-children, followed by the townspeople, snakes around the village. Celebrations are usually rounded off with some fireworks, the louder the bang the better. The following list is a guide:

Paleokastritsa (Fri. after Easter); Analipsis (Ascension Day); Lakones and Kastellani (Whit Sunday); Nymphes (21 May); Gouvia (12 June); Petreli (2 July); Agios Prokopios and Kavos (8 July); Magoulades (20 July); Mount Pantocrator (3-6 Aug.); Pontikonissi (6 Aug.); Mandouki (14 Aug.); Myrtiotissa (24 Sep.).

See **Culture**.

Ferries: The port terminal has few facilities but there are toilets and a bureau de change, tel: 30481. The ticket agencies are ranged along Zavitsianou and Donzelot, below the Old Town, facing the Old Port, and along Xenofontos Stratigou below the New Fort. The port police have kiosks at both the Old and New ports.

Hellenic Mediterranean Lines, tel: 39747, runs services to Brindisi and Patras; Corfu-Saudi Travel, 46 Xenofontos Stratigou, tel: 25003, runs services to Brindisi, Ancona, Bari and Venice; Ionian Lines, Epirus Lines and Fragline are at 74, 76 and 50 Xenofontos Stratigou; Vikentios Manessis Travel, tel: 32664. There are also services from Kavos on the south coast to Paxos at 0930 Mon., Tue., Fri. and Sat. See **ISLANDS**.

Food: For a quick snack try *oukoumaes* (doughnuts), *typoites* (cheese pies), sausage rolls, *anakoites* (spinach pies) and pizzas, all from bakeries. Starters include tzatziki (cucumber and yoghurt with garlic and herbs) and taramasalata (fish roe dip), which are eaten with bread and ideally a glass of ouzo (see **Drinks**). For a main course try moussaka (minced lamb, aubergines, potatoes and béchamel sauce); souvlakia (chunks of pork or lamb barbecued on a skewer); pastitsio (minced meat, macaroni and béchamel sauce); or *stifado* (beef casseroled with wine and onions). Specialities from Corfu include: *sofrito* (veal casserole in white sauce seasoned with onions and garlic); *bourdeto* (fish casserole with onions and red pepper); and *pastitsada* (veal cooked in tomato sauce with pasta). Fish is always fresh and available everywhere, cooked over charcoal, fried or in soup. Try the more exotic seafood such as octopus, squid and crispy fried *calamari*. Lobster is delicious but very expensive. See **RESTAURANTS 1 & 2**, **Eating Out**.

Guides: The Association of Guides, tel: 37847, will provide a guide who speaks any language to take you where you want to go. Alternatively, make arrangements with a trusted taxi driver who knows his way around, or book up with an organized tour which should have a multilingual guide. Guidebooks are available in most European languages at bookshops in Corfu Town (see **SHOPPING 2**).

Health: Visitors are strongly advised to take out personal medical insurance before leaving home. Residents of EC countries are treated free (UK residents should obtain form E111 from the Department of Social Security before travelling abroad).
General hospital (with 24 hr emergency service): Aghia Irini, Konstanta Street, tel: 45811 (5 lines). Ambulances are prompt and efficient.
Clinic: 1 Ethniki Paleokastritsa, tel: 22946.
English-speaking doctor: Thanasis Michalopoulos, 23a I. Theotoki Street, tel: 37540/34206.
English-speaking dentist: Michalis Valmas, 9 Evangelistrias, tel: 30458. In general, standards of hygiene on the island are good. Fair-skinned visitors should take care at first in the sun, particularly in the summer. Many inexperienced riders are involved in accidents on hired mopeds and motorcycles, so take care. See **Chemists**, **Insurance**.

Insurance: You are advised to take out comprehensive holiday insurance. If you are taken ill or have an accident and need treatment or repatriation, this can be extremely expensive. See **Crime & Theft**, **Driving**, **Health**.

Laundries: The hotel laundry service may take 2-3 days in high season, but there are a number of Launderettes in the resort towns which offer service washes or do-it-yourself facilities.

Lost Property: The only lost-property office is Lost and Found at the airport, tel: 33576.

Markets: The only market is north of San Rocco Square. It is the cheapest place to buy fruit and vegetables if you are self-catering and is an interesting place to wander through for a taste of Corfu life. On village saints' days (see **Events**) you will find stalls set up in the streets selling food and souvenirs. See **Shopping**.

Money: A passport is usually necessary when changing money. Traveller's cheques, Eurocheques and cash can be exchanged for drachmas at banks and bureaux de change (which have longer opening hours). Banks have no commission charges but bureaux de change will make a charge of about 2%. Some hotels and tour operators will offer to cash traveller's cheques but the rate of exchange will not be particularly favourable. Larger shops in Corfu Town will accept traveller's cheques. Major credit cards (MasterCard, Visa, American Express) are only accepted by the more up-market shops in Corfu Town, by the luxury hotels, by the international car hire companies and by the larger petrol stations near Corfu Town. Very few rural petrol stations accept credit cards or traveller's cheques, and nor do most restaurants, private hotels or small shops.

National Bank of Greece, Voulgareos Street, Corfu Town, tel: 38597; Commerical Bank of Greece, Voulgareos Street, Corfu Town, tel: 39636; Credit Bank of Greece, 4 Agios Dimitriou Street, Corfu Town, tel: 38111. See **Currency, Opening Times.**

Music: Brass bands perform at the Bandstand at the south end of the Esplanade on summer Sat. around 2100. You will also hear them at parades for village saints' days and other events (see **A-Z**). Bouzouki music is thriving and there are several clubs where you can hear the best players from the Greek mainland, as well as local performers (see

Achillion Palace

NIGHTLIFE, **Bouzouki**). The Corfu Festival takes place every Sep.-Oct., with ballet, opera and classical music performed by local and visiting companies. See **Culture**.

Newspapers: Foreign newspapers and periodicals are available one day after publication in kiosks and shops all over Corfu. Two English-language newspapers printed in Greece are *Athens News*, a daily with Greek and world news and television listings, and *Corfu News*, a free monthly newspaper (April-Oct.), which carries events listings with up-to-date information. The *Corfu Messenger* comes out weekly, covering local news, with adverts, a horoscope, and theatre, cinema, television and radio listings. There are also *The Corfiot* and *The Corfu Sun*. See **What's On**.

Nightlife: There is plenty to do at night in Corfu, from sitting at a pavement café, sipping a cool drink and watching the world go by, to taking part in organized outings. There are several widely available deals, e.g. to Danilia Village and Korakiana, which offer transport, food, wine and entertainment for a very reasonable inclusive price. There is also a range of discos, from the small bar with a dance floor to the huge and sophisticated establishments along 'The Strip' (Ethnikis

Antistasis) on the way out of Corfu Town to the north. Each resort also has a selection whose popularity swings with the seasons. There is usually only a small entry fee to pay, money being made on the price of the drinks, which can be quite high. There are three cinemas in Corfu Town which show English and European films with Greek subtitles: Pallas, G. Theotoki Street; Orpheus, Akadimias; and Nausika, Marasali (open air). There is a casino at the Corfu Hilton Hotel – take your passport and wear evening dress. See **NIGHTLIFE**.

Opening Times:
Banks – 0800-1400, 1615-1800 or 1730-1945 Mon.-Fri.
Chemists – 0815-1330 Mon.-Sat., 1715-2030 Tue., Thu. & Fri. Other times on rota basis: ask at your hotel or tel: 30265.
Shops – 0800-1300, 1700-2030 Tue., Thu. & Fri. Many shops stay open all day every day during the high season.

Orientation: Corfu is 50 km long from north to south and at its widest point 27 km from east to west. It has a population of approximately 100,000, almost one-third of whom live in Corfu Town, known locally as Kerkyra, the only sizable town on the island. It is a busy commercial centre, but the fascinating Old Town is a mass of quiet, winding streets punctuated with gracious buildings which echo stages of the history of the island. The northern end of the island is mountainous – the peak of Mount Pantocrator is over 900 m – and Kassiopi on the northeast tip has an historic harbour. The northwest corner has dramatic sandstone rock formations and extensive sandy beaches. The south is generally lower and the resorts of Benitses, Messonghi and Kavos are very popular. The west coast beaches are the longest and least developed.

Parking: Parking in the narrow, often one-way streets of Corfu Town is quite impossible. Park along the front by the Old and New ports, below the New Fort. In other parts of the island parking is not a problem. Restricted parking is marked by wide yellow lines and signs in English. In theory illegal parking results in a fine or the removal of numberplates, which can be difficult to retrieve; should this occur, contact the tourist police. See **Driving**.

Passports & Customs: A visa is not required to enter Corfu but a valid passport is essential for a stay of up to three months (citizens of non-EC countries may be subject to some restrictions; enquire at travel agents). To extend the length of your stay, apply to the Aliens Bureau, tel: 39494, or at the Greek embassy in your home country. No vaccination certificates are needed unless you are travelling from a country with a known epidemic. There are no restrictions on the import of foreign currency, but if you wish to leave with a large sum of money it must have been declared on arrival, or you must have documents proving you received the money from outside the country during the course of your stay (apply to a bank for information). See **Customs Allowances**.

Petrol: Super, unleaded and diesel are available at all stations, with prices similar to those in the UK. You will be served. There is at least one station in most resorts but few in between, so make sure you have a full tank before embarking on any excursions into the backwoods. Fuel stations usually close at 1900 and are often closed on Sun. Few take credit cards or traveller's cheques. See **Driving**.

Police: The tourist police (at the entrance to New Fortress Square, Corfu Town, tel: 30265) wear a pale grey uniform and are responsible for visitors' problems with accommodation, prices, etc. The security police, 19 Alexandra Street, Corfu Town, tel: 37696/22340, appear more military and take care of car accidents, theft, drug offences, etc. They ride motorcycles and have patrol cars. See **Crime & Theft**, **Emergency Numbers**.

Post Offices: The central post office is in Alexandras Avenue, Corfu Town, and is open 0730-2000. Facilities include a poste restante service, stamps and currency exchange. Leave packets and registered letters open as the clerk will want to check the contents. Postboxes are yellow, and stamps may also be purchased at the shop where you buy your cards, and at some kiosks.

Public Holidays: 1 Jan.; 6 Jan. (Epiphany); 1st day of Lent; 25 Mar. (Independence Day); Good Fri.; Easter Sun.; Easter Mon.; 1 May (Labour

Day); Whit Mon.; 21 May (Enosis Day, Ionian islands only); 11 Aug. (St. Spiridon Procession); 15 Aug. (Assumption); 28 Oct. (Ochi Day); 25 Dec.; 26 Dec.

Rabies: Corfu is officially rabies-free, but any animal bites should be seen to immediately by a doctor.

Religious Services:
Roman Catholic – Church in Town Hall Square. Sun. and holiday Masses: 0730, 0830, 1000 & 1900 June-Sep., 0900, 1000 & 1800 Oct.-May. Daily at 0800.
Judaism – Synagogue, Odos Paleologou, Corfu Town.
Anglican – 21 Mavili Street, Corfu Town: 1030 Sun.

Shopping: Most resorts now have outlets for souvenirs such as jewellery or leather work, but for the best selection head for N. Theotoki, Voulgareos and surrounding streets in Corfu Town. Prices are generally clearly marked but they are not carved in stone, particularly if you are prepared to pay in cash and if you buy more than one item. However, be polite and understand that a living has to be made. In the height of the season, shops which are dependent on the tourist trade may stay open all day. Otherwise, there is a break for lunch 1330-1630. See SHOPPING 1 & 2, **Best Buys**, **Markets**, **Opening Times**.

Smoking: There is officially no smoking on buses or in public buildings such as cinemas, theatres and museums. Restaurants rarely have restrictions but you can usually sit outdoors to escape.

Sports: A growing number of sports facilities are available around the island. Many of the bigger hotels have squash and tennis courts, and there is a tennis club in Corfu Town (Polila Street, off Vraila Street, near the Archaeological Museum).
Cricket: The game was brought to the island by the British in 1864 and is very popular. The main pitch is on the Spianada in Corfu Town and matches are played here on Wed. and Sun., starting 1500. There are two clubs and a cricket festival in Sep., with teams from England and Malta.

Cricket, Corfu Town

Golf: Corfu Golf and Country Club is at Ermones in the Ropa Valley (PO Box 71, 49100 Corfu, tel: 94220) and offers 18 holes over a length of 6803 yd on a very attractive course. Equipment can be hired (1500 Drs for a half-set of clubs) and lessons received.

Horse-riding: Contact Mr Dimitrius at Kerkyra Golf, tel: 31785/6. There is also a stable just outside Roda; call in and book.
See **Water Sports**.

Taxis: There are several taxi ranks in Corfu Town: at the Old Port, on G. Theotoki Street, on the Esplanade and at San Rocco Square. Taxis do have meters but it is more common to arrange a price before you set off. This is the best way to avoid arguments. Reliable radio taxis can be called to any part of the island, tel: 33811/33812/41333. See **Tipping**.

Telephones & Telegrams: Calls can be made from OTE (Greek Telecommunications Organization) offices. The main office (24 hr service) is at 3 Mantzarou Street, behind the central post office. Wait in the queue and you will be allocated a booth; you pay when you come out. Cheap rates are after 2100 and at weekends. Telephone boxes are all operated by telephone cards, which can be purchased at the airport stationers and at OTE offices. The code for Corfu Town for outside callers is 0661. International dialling codes from Corfu: UK 0044, USA

001, Canada 001, Australia 0061, New Zealand 0064, Republic of Ireland 00353. To obtain a reversed-charge call, contact the operator by dialling 161 for a call outside Europe or 151 for Europe (facility available Mon.-Fri.). Tel: 162 for an English-speaking operator. Telegrams can be sent from OTE offices or tel: 155. See **Emergency Numbers**.

Television & Radio: The national Greek radio stations are: ERT 1st programme (1008 KHz/91.80 MHz) – daily weather forecast and sea conditions in English at 0630, and news in English, French, German and Arabic at 0740; ERT2 (981 KHz) – news in English and French at 1420 and 2120; ERT 2nd programme (93.80 MHz) – music, both Greek and foreign; and ERT 3rd programme (666 KHz) – classical music. Two TV channels, ERT1 and ERT2, operate 1730-2400 Mon.-Fri. and 1100-0100 Sat. and Sun., and occasionally show American, English and German films.

Time Difference: Corfu is 2 hr ahead of BST and GMT.

Tipping: Service is always included in restaurant and hotel bills, although it is also customary to tip the chambermaid or waiter if you are satisfied with the service. Taxi drivers, waiters and hairdressers are normally tipped 10%; chambermaids 500 Drs a week; porters 200 Drs.

Toilets: There are public toilets on San Rocco Square and at the edge of the Esplanade opposite the Olympic Airways office (the attendant will expect a tip of 100 Drs), although visitors are recommended to use the toilets in bars and cafés whenever possible.

Tourist Information: The NTOG (National Tourist Office of Greece) is at the entrance to New Fortress Square. English is spoken and information can be given on the telephone, tel: 37520. Advice is given on accommodation and activities, and you can pick up free maps, newspapers, timetables and a cultural programme. In the UK, contact the Greek Tourist Information Office at 4 Conduit Street, London W1R 0DJ, tel: 071-7345997. See **Guides**, **What's On**.

Transport: See **Airport**, **Buses**, **Ferries**, **Taxis**.

A-Z

Traveller's Cheques: See **Money**.

Water Sports: Pedalos, canoes, wind-surfers, jetskis, water-skiing, ring rides and paragliding are available at most of the larger resorts. Scuba diving is popular in the clear waters: Mike's Diving at Paleokastritsa and Aqua Club on the Old Port waterfront in Corfu Town will help with equipment and compressed air. Diving trips are arranged by some operators, at about 8000 Drs per day, including gear. Bare boat and skippered yacht charter is available at Kontokali Marina; Smart Yachts is run by an English couple, tel: 91786; and Zante and Regal Yachting offer day sails with lunch (0830-1800), and evening sails (1930-2330), including dinner and wine. See **Sports**, **Yachts**.

What's On: Corfu is a small island so if there is anything unusual going on you will get to hear about it. Flyposters are the most common form of advertising and it is worth keeping an eye open for these. The *Corfu News* and *Messenger* (see **Newspapers**) carry listings of events, and Radio Rama (96.3 FM) broadcasts in English, including a calendar of events, 1500-1700 Mon.-Sat. See **Culture**, **Events**, **Tourist Information**.

Yachts: Yachts entering Greek waters for the first time must make themselves known to the Port Authority, tel: 30481. The best, safest and newest marina is at Kontokali, 5 km north of Corfu Town. Fresh water and electricity are available, and local shops offer a free grocery delivery service. For equipment the main chandlers are along X. Stratigou behind the Old Port, Corfu Town.

Youth Hostels: There is an international youth hostel at Kontokali, tel: 91202. Bring your YHA card or join at the hostel.

This book was produced using QuarkXPress™ and
Adobe Illustrator 3.2™ on Apple Macintosh™
computers and output to separated film on a
Linotronic™ 300 Imagesetter

Text: Hilary Hughes, with additional
information by William McDowall
Photography: Neil Wilson
Electronic Cartography: Susan Harvey Design,
and Iain Robinson (1, 18, 34, 52)

First published 1990 Second Edition 1994
Copyright © HarperCollins Publishers
Published by HarperCollins Publishers
Printed in Italy by Amadeus S.p.A.
ISBN 0 00 470487-8